LEMONGRASS AND LIME

First published in Great Britain by Simon & Schuster UK Ltd., 2000

A Kirsty Melville Book

1⊜
Ten Speed Press
P.O. Box 7123
Berkeley, CA 94707
www.tenspeed.com

Distributed in Canada by Ten Speed Press Canada.

Library of Congress Cataloging-in-Publication data is on file with the publisher.

ISBN 1-58008-321-8

First U.S. Printing, 2001
Printed in Singapore

1 2 3 4 5 6 7 8 9 10 — 05 04 03 02 01

LEMONGRASS AND LIME

NEW VIETNAMESE COOKING

PREFACE BY MOGENS THOLSTRUP

RECIPES BY MARK READ | PHOTOGRAPHS BY JEAN CAZALS

TEN SPEED PRESS
Berkeley • Toronto

▪ *All recipes serve four unless otherwise stated.*

preface

The idea for Bam-Bou came to me long before I had ever been to Vietnam, but it was during my trip there that it all began to fall into place, from the type of food we would serve down to the decor. My first clue as to how the Vietnamese cook and eat came from my man in Saigon: "The Vietnamese are like most Asian people - very clean and fussy about freshness of their food," he explained. "When they do their shopping they tend to buy food in the exact quantities needed to cook for their next meal. They might buy one carrot and two onions at the market for lunch, only to return to the same stall later that day to buy the same for dinner. They are, of course, from the same carrot and onion stall as earlier, but this does not seem to make any difference."

As I began to explore the restaurants, cafés, and markets of Saigon, the full range of Vietnamese cooking styles became apparent. In one restaurant diners grilled their own meat on an earthenware fire that the waiter brought to the table. We had beef, pork, frog's legs, and whole sparrow. The Chonon market in the Chinese district exceeded anything I had ever seen in terms of exotic fruit, vegetables, spices, live animals, seafood, and things I had never thought were meant for human consumption. Later the same day at lunch, I was served a delicious selection of noodles, spring rolls, and fried pork.

At a lovely restaurant called 3-Mien I was introduced to food from Hue, the old imperial city. The food from Hue is even more delicate than from the rest of the country. We started with an exquisite salad of chopped fresh bamboo shoots and prawns, followed by a caramelized fish that was equally delicious. The Mandarin, despite the Chinese sounding name, also served Hue food. The dish that really blew me away consisted of a minced prawn mix tucked inside a delicate rice paper parcel with sesame seeds on top, which had been pan-fried. Tiny scallops with ginger were also very good as was a fish dish called Cha-Ka that was cooked with dill, which I was too full to appreciate. Here I had experienced perhaps the best food of the whole trip – and it set the standard for the menu at Bam-Bou.

Mogens Tholstrup

introduction

"One eats exceedingly well in Saigon. The cooks are practically artists, very learned in their art. They prepare the dishes with pleasure and the slowness of good omen."

NOTES SUR LA VIE FRANCAISE EN COCHINCHINE, PIERRE NICOLAS, 1778

Vietnamese cuisine is light, subtle, and elegant. It is a simple yet sophisticated style of cooking characterized by fresh, clean tastes, by the delicate blending of spicy and sweet, and by seductive tropical aromas. Grilled beef is paired with tart raw papaya, and pungent shrimp paste with sweet sugar cane. A sprinkling of crispy deep-fried shallots or roasted peanuts contrasts with soft rice noodles, while diced red chiles and chives garnish a bowl of sweet and sour fish soup. Above all, Vietnamese cuisine is about balance – balance of flavors and fragrance, of texture and of color. A dish should be as pleasing to the eye and nose as it is to the palate.

Vietnamese food is frequently described as a fusion of Chinese and Thai. In fact it is far more complex. There are discernible regional differences as well as major contributions from India and, more recently, France. This definition also fails to convey the cuisine's several unique characteristics. The Vietnamese have absorbed particular culinary traditions from their neighbours and erstwhile rulers – mainly ingredients, implements, and techniques but also elements of their philosophical approaches to cooking – to create something entirely their own. No other Southeast Asian cuisine displays such delicacy nor such subtle blending of flavors.

Vietnam is a long, thin, S-shaped country, which its inhabitants are fond of comparing to a bamboo carrying pole flexing under the weight of two rice panniers at either end. These baskets represent the all-important rice-lands of the Mekong and Red River deltas; while the pole in between is a narrow, rather arid coastal strip backed by rugged mountains. It was the Chinese who introduced wet-rice cultivation to Vietnam some four thousand years ago. The grain is now Vietnam's staple food, consumed as plain steamed rice, noodles, vinegar, crackers, wrappers, sweetmeats, and alcohol. Rice also lies at the heart of Vietnamese culture. It is a sacred food, the stuff of legend: rice cakes are offered to the gods

opposite: *peeled citrus fruits*

and placed on ancestral altars, while special "Heaven and Earth" cakes made of glutinous-rice flour are central to celebrations surrounding Tet, the Vietnamese New Year. For much of the rural population, the year follows the rhythm of the rice harvest.

Fish and fish products provide the other great unifier of Vietnamese cuisine. Not only are there hundreds of different types of seafood, but also fresh water species in abundance from paddy fields, village ponds, lakes, and mountain streams. Shrimps are pounded into powders and pastes; diaphanous dried baby squid hang on snack stalls; at markets, soft-shell crabs lie in spiky bundles next to buckets full of eels and myriad rainbow-colored fish. Vietnam's most distinctive and ubiquitous sauce, nuoc mam, is made from fermented salted anchovies. Though it is an acquired taste, more pungent than other fish sauces of the region, nuoc mam never clashes but blends almost imperceptibly into other flavors. It is used much as soy sauce in China for both seasoning and flavoring, and it also provides the basis for countless marinades, dressings, and dipping sauces. Mixed with chiles, sugar, lime, and rice vinegar, for example, nuoc mam becomes nuoc cham. This is another quintessential Vietnamese taste – at once spicy, sour, and salty-sweet, yet never harsh. It appears on the table in some guise or another at almost every meal.

Most Vietnamese meals also feature a platter of raw vegetables, fresh salad greens, or herbs. A typical combination might include one of several local varieties of mint or basil, lettuce, sliced green banana, and star fruit, perhaps rounded off with finely shredded banana flower. Lettuce leaves, or sometimes rice papers, are often used to wrap crispy spring rolls, bite-sized morsels of steamed fish, or barbecued meat with herbs to make a flavor-filled package which is then dipped in the accompanying sauce. Each mouthful releases an explosion of different tastes and aromas.

Where meat is used in cooking in Vietnam it appears in small quantities – a reflection of its scarcity in a rice-growing country where fish and soy products have traditionally provided protein. Chicken, duck, and pork are the most commonly eaten meats, mixed into stir-fries and soups or minced in sausages, while beef has always been considered a luxury. In pho bo, north Vietnam's classic noodle soup, a few, almost transparent beef slices are added just before serving to cook in the aromatic stock. Fresh ingredients are

opposite & below right: *incense and fresh produce at a street market*

vital to a cuisine where flavor and texture are everything. This means that, even in big Vietnamese cities, produce comes from the farmer, fisherman, or butcher to the consumer in less than a day.

Many cooks buy in sufficient quantities for only one meal, even if this means shopping two or three times a day, from hawkers who roam the streets or from neighborhood markets. Such a demand for fresh produce, coupled with poorly developed transport systems, partly explains the regional variations in Vietnamese cuisine. The other reasons are historical.

The Sweet and Sour Flavors of China

For a thousand years northern Vietnam was ruled by China. It is here, not surprisingly, that Chinese influence on the cuisine is at its strongest, though over the centuries much has also diffused southwards. In addition to chopsticks and the wok, the Chinese introduced rice noodles, tofu, star anise, and soy sauce to Vietnamese kitchens. The idea of combining and balancing flavours originally came from China, as did sausages and sweet and sour soups. In the thirteenth century the Mongols left behind a taste for beef and hot pots following a series of unsuccessful invasions. Nevertheless, even in northern Vietnam there are significant differences between local and Chinese cuisine. One of the most noticeable is that tastes are cleaner and fresher, the food lighter and easier to digest. In general, dishes are more likely to be grilled, steamed, simmered, barbecued, or braised than fried, but when they do fry, Vietnamese cooks use far less oil than

Chinese, and rarely use thickening agents. Individual flavors are more prominent, as is the use of fragrant herbs and raw vegetables, which never appear on Chinese tables.

Thanks to a cooler climate, food in the north is also less varied than in southern and central Vietnam. Dishes tend to be less spicy – black pepper and galangal are more in evidence than chiles – and warming stews, soups, and rice gruels are served more often. Pho bo is a typical northern soup, combining a flavorful beef and ginger stock with rice noodles, onions, and fragrant basil. Crunchy bean sprouts, chopped red chiles, and a squeeze of fresh lime add further texture and a dash of color in addition to a hot-sour taste. As with many traditional Vietnamese dishes, pho bo is street food. The best is eaten at makeshift kitchens where diners squat on pint-size stools around a steaming cauldron. Another popular northern street food is bun cha. This highly aromatic dish of pork-meat sausages is served on a bed of cold rice vermicelli noodles in a thin sour-sweet sauce and accompanied by a side plate of herbs and salad greens. Both bun cha and pho bo have spread throughout Vietnam, while the more recently invented and refined cha ca is still found in only a few specialist restaurants. In cha ca marinated morsels of firm-textured fish are fried at the table, with chopped spring onions and generous amounts of dill providing an unforgettable aroma.

Spices from India

While northern Vietnam came under Chinese sway, the south was ruled by various Indian-influenced kingdoms, including the Khmer, before being absorbed into Vietnam. This, combined with the greater variety of vegetables, fish, tropical fruits, herbs, and spices available, allows southern cooks a far wider repertoire. Overall, southerners prefer their food spicier than in the north. They have a fondness for curries and hot dipping sauces, though nothing like the fiery heat of Thai food, which would overpower the subtle flavor combinations at the heart of Vietnamese cuisine. Instead, coconut milk and sugar are used to smooth and sweeten.

One of the south's archetypal dishes is chao tom – minced shrimp meat grilled on a sugar-cane skewer – in which a light, natural sweetness enhances the fish flavors. Fruit is also much in evidence, both to complement savory dishes and as the most common form of dessert, from bananas, mangoes, mangosteen, and papaya to the lovely but unusual dragon fruit – a speciality of Nha Trang. The food of central Vietnam, a culinary transition zone, shares many similarities with both north and south. The one notable exception is Hue. This city, the former imperial capital of Vietnam, is renowned for its sophisticated and inventive cooking, which takes the Vietnamese contrast of textures, color, and flavor

opposite: pho bo soup   **below right:** *horseradish*

to new heights. The epitome of this is Hue's imperial cuisine, comprising an array of small but elaborate, eye-catching dishes. Developed in the nineteenth century, it is now experiencing a revival, thanks largely to the tourist trade, though such elegant fare is out of the reach of ordinary people. In general Hue food is more complex and labor-intensive, with presentation more important than in other regions. One of the city's most famous dishes is banh khoai, a small, crispy yellow pancake folded over a shrimp, pork, and bean sprout stuffing, which is then dipped in a peanut and sesame sauce. Hue cooks wrap small pieces of grilled beef in pungent leaves and shrimps in tiny, semi-translucent pancakes. Whole shrimps, sliced pork and spices go inside the tapioca flour pancake, which is then steamed in a banana leaf to make a delicate parcel. The accompanying dipping sauce is pepped up with a dash of chile.

French Impressions

Towards the end of the nineteenth century, at the same time as the emperors were enjoying their imperial banquets, Vietnam was gradually being colonized by the French. They were by no means the first or only Europeans to arrive on Vietnamese shores, however. From the sixteenth century onwards, Portuguese and Spanish traders sailed into Hoi An, quickly followed by the English, Dutch, and French. In return for local pepper, cinnamon, musk, and silk, among other goods, the Europeans traded a number of fruits and vegetables, many of them from the recently discovered New World. Potatoes, tomatoes, corn, peanuts, chile pepper, and cauliflower all arrived in Vietnam on European ships. The local names for several foods still indicate this European connection: snow peas are known as Dutch beans; turkey as Western chicken; and asparagus as Western bamboo shoots. Many of these new foods thrived in the cool uplands around Da Lat, an area that to this day produces a vast range of fruits and vegetables, from carrots, fennel, leeks, and lettuces to avocados, plums, and intensely sweet strawberries.

opposite: *rice-stuffed banana leaves*

Among all the Europeans, though, it was the French who left the strongest impression on Vietnam – especially its cuisine. Apart from asparagus and a taste for white potatoes, French colonists brought artichokes, pears, and grapes packed on ice for the long sea journey before growing them locally. During nearly a century of colonial power they introduced dairy products, including butter, yogurt, and ice cream, as well as omelets, frog's legs, steak, and dill. They taught Vietnamese cooks how to make French bread, custard tarts, croissants, and pain au chocolat, and how to rustle up a crème caramel or crêpe suzette. Coffee drinking gradually became part of the Vietnamese way of life, while milk tea even became popular in some circles. Such was the French influence on Saigon, today's Ho Chi Minh City, that it was known as the Paris of the Orient.

Despite the intervening wars and years of hardline Communist rule, French influence is still apparent in Vietnam. The majority of top-class restaurants serve French-style food, often in beautifully renovated colonial villas, while specialty stores sell French wine, cheese, and charcuterie. Warm, crusty baguettes are sold on street corners and delicious, plump croissants in almost every cafè. As ingredients improve and demand increases, Vietnamese chefs are beginning to reintroduce old, almost-forgotten recipes and also to experiment with new techniques and flavors in time-honored fashion. At the same time Vietnamese cuisine is becoming more popular abroad, particularly in America and France, but also elsewhere.

Modern Vietnamese Cooking

In creating the recipes for this book, Mark Read, the head chef of London's Bam-Bou restaurant, has fashioned a modern Vietnamese cuisine. Though his inspiration is firmly rooted in classical dishes, from traditional street food to the more elaborate fare of French colonial Vietnam, Mark has reinvented them for contemporary tastes. In doing so he brings a fresh approach to the ingredients while never losing sight of the essentials: the unique blend of delicate and diverse tastes, the balance of natural aromas and the sophisticated texture combinations at the heart of the Vietnamese style of cooking. In the Bam-Bou kitchen you will find the seductive flavors of lemongrass, dill, and chile contrasted with the clean tastes of steamed, grilled, or braised meats and seafoods. The heady perfumes of aromatic herbs

opposite: *green beans and red chiles*

are paired with crisp raw vegetables and the sharp sweetness of citrus fruits. This is modern Vietnamese cooking at its best – subtle, varied, healthy, and packed with flavor.

The dishes in *Lemongrass and Lime* are simple in conception and easy to prepare. They focus on fresh, quality ingredients which are readily available in major supermarkets or from specialty Asian and Caribbean grocers. For those ingredients that may prove more difficult to find – such as kaffir limes and Chinese chives – suitable alternatives are given wherever possible in the ingredients list on page 26. The basic tools required are non-stick frying pans, a wok for stir-frying – which gives better all round heat and is easier to handle than conventional pans – and a sharp knife with a very clean cut.

A typical Vietnamese meal consists of several shared dishes all brought to the table at once. At its simplest it will include rice, a vegetable, and a fish, or possibly meat dish and soup. Small bowls of nuoc cham or some other dipping sauce are provided, sometimes with a plate of lime wedges, which are squeezed over a pepper and salt mix to create a tangy condiment. A few chopped chiles might also be added to taste. Diners then help themselves to small amounts of each dish – one at a time in order to savor the individual flavors. They place a portion of one dish into their individual bowls of rice and eat this before trying the next dish. The soup is usually consumed toward the end of a meal, before dessert, but can be used to offer a cleansing break between starter and main courses.

Finally, when planning a meal, try to select a range of dishes with contrasting colors, textures, and flavors. For example, a spicy stir-fry could be served with soft noodles or a sour-sweet dish with crunchy vegetables and a side-plate of fragrant greens. Vietnamese food is traditionally accompanied by weak green tea, jasmine tea, or rice wine, though cold beer and some lighter wines would go equally well.

ingredients

"There were wayside food-stalls everywhere, and as

much attention, one felt sure, was paid to the matching

of the colors of the food displayed in the bowls,

as to the flavor itself."

The Dragon Apparent, Norman Lewis, *1951*

ingredients

Asian basil Among the many different varieties of basil, this one is best recognized by its pungent aniseed aroma, glossy green leaf, and purple stem. It is not always easy to find, even at specialty stores, but unfortunately there is no really good alternative; Mediterranean basil definitely lacks the required intensity of flavor and fragrance. Asian basil is an essential ingredient of Pho Bo, Vietnam's famous breakfast soup (see page 68), and is also used for balancing the hot flavors of dishes such as Spicy Herbed Leaf Salad or Spicy Raw Beef (see pages 93 and 131). In most cases the leaves are either eaten raw in salads or as a garnish, or added right at the end of the cooking process in order to preserve their color and aroma. As with any basil, look for firm stems of healthy green leaves. They will turn black if chopped roughly, so either shred them by hand or use a very sharp knife.

Bean sprouts These days fresh bean sprouts, generally of the mung bean, are widely available in supermarkets and specialty grocers. When buying them avoid sprouts that are discolored, and be careful to handle them as little as possible since the fragile stalks are easily bruised. Though bean sprouts can be kept for one or two days in the fridge (in an air-tight container rather than a bag), it is best to use them as quickly as possible after purchase. Preparation consists of simply rinsing them under cold water. Whether you also remove each brown, hairy root and any remaining green husks is purely a matter of preference. Beans sprouts are best eaten raw or only very lightly cooked to make the most of their subtle, nutty flavor and crunchy texture. They add a fresh, almost sweet aroma to stir-fries, but overcooking renders the sprouts watery, so add them only at the very last minute, almost as a garnish. For the Chicken and Cashew Stir-Fry (see page 137), for example, toss the sprouts just a couple of times in the pan before serving. If fresh bean sprouts are not available, avoid the canned variety, which lacks the essential crunchiness. Instead, it is not difficult to sprout your own. Soak the required amount of mung beans overnight in sufficient water to cover, then drain and place on a damp kitchen towel in large glass jars or plastic containers. Cover the beans with another damp kitchen towel and leave them somewhere warm and dark. Two or three times a day remove the top towel, sprinkle the beans with fresh, slightly tepid water, and drain off any excess. After a day or so the beans should start sending down roots, and should be large enough to use by the fourth or fifth day. Before use, plunge the sprouts in a bowl of cold water, allowing any loose husks to float to the surface.

opposite: *Chinese chives*

Black fungus mushroom Also known as wood ear, cloud ear, or tree ear, this Chinese mushroom is usually sold in its dried form. It is easily recognizable by its thin, frilly cap, velvety black coloring on top and beige underneath. To prepare black fungus mushrooms, pour boiling water over them and leave to stand for five to ten minutes, then drain, sluicing out any grit. Finally, remove the stem (if present) and any hard portions of the cap which will now have expanded considerably. With its delicate, earthy flavor and chunky texture, black fungus adds structure to Crispy Spring Rolls (see page 74) and is also a favorite for soups and stir-fries, though beware of overcooking.

Bok choy Bok choy is a type of Chinese cabbage commonly available at Asian stores. Confusingly, there are many different varieties with similar or even identical names. Vietnamese bok choy is smaller and broader than the Chinese variety, looking more like a paler version of pak choy (see page 41). In fact bok choy and pak choy are largely interchangeable, the main differences being that bok choy is brighter green, a touch more crispy in texture, and has a slightly sweeter, less peppery taste. If you can find it, tender baby bok choy is the best. Depending on their size, bok choy leaves can be used whole or chopped as desired. You can use just the raw stems, shredded finely, to make a crispy bed of fragrant greens for the Crispy Smoked Chicken with Fragrant Greens (see page 128). The whole leaf, however, goes into Wok-Seared Greens (see page 86) and Chicken and Cashew Stir-Fry (see page 137) – in both cases it is color and texture that you are after so take care not to overcook. For a simple vegetable dish, boil bok choy in salted water then toss it with liberal quantities of oyster sauce (see below).

Chinese chives The heads of Chinese chives provide a truly exotic garnish as each thick, green stem, up to around eight inches long, is topped with a pale yellow conical bud. The whole chive can be chopped into salads – imparting a garlicky onion tang – or used to flavor soups and stir-fries. Cut the stems with scissors or a sharp knife into half-inch-long segments to avoid excessive bruising. When buying Chinese chives, look for stems that snap rather than bend and a plump, closed bud. Flowering buds become rather too fibrous to eat, but can still be used as an attractive garnish. It should be possible to find Chinese chives in specialty stores. If not, substitute with double the quantities of regular chives.

opposite: *fish sauce is an essential condiment*

Coconut milk Coconut in all its forms features prominently in southern Vietnamese cuisine. The delicately perfumed milk is used to smooth and sweeten otherwise fiery curries and in refreshing drinks, while the candied flesh is a constituent of many festive sweetmeats. Even the local version of crème caramel, introduced by the French, is made with coconut milk. The milk is used in Sweet Coconut Rice (see page 157) and Grilled Salmon with Coconut Curry (see page 113). To extract coconut milk, the flesh (or unsweetened desiccated coconut can be used instead) is blended with a little water and then squeezed. However, excellent-quality milk is also available frozen or in cans – try to find an unsweetened variety. Any leftover milk will keep in the fridge for up to one week in a sealed container, not in the can as this leaves an unpleasant taste. When cooking with coconut milk, avoid adding it to boiling sauces or letting it overheat since the milk has a tendency to curdle at high temperatures.

Fish sauce A clear, amber-colored liquid made from fermented salted anchovies, Vietnamese fish sauce is something of an acquired taste. The best sauce, which is graded like olive oil, comes from Phu Quoc island and Phan Thiet in southern Vietnam, where fresh anchovies are layered with salt in wooden vats and left to ferment for six months. The resulting nutrient-rich liquid is bottled for use at the table as a pouring sauce and basic condiment. A second "pressing" is obtained by adding water to the vat and applying a weight; this lower-grade sauce is reserved primarily for the kitchen. Despite its salty pungency, fish sauce used in the right quantity adds a surprisingly sophisticated note to all manner of dishes, blending and enhancing rather than standing out as a single identifiable flavor. Nevertheless, it is perhaps best to start with fairly conservative amounts and build according to taste. Fish sauce provides the base ingredient for a vast array of dressings, marinades and dipping sauces. Combined with chile, lemon juice, and sugar it is known as nuoc cham (see page 38), while its salty tang provides balance to Ginger Dressing (see page 59) and complements the sweetness of Caramelized Ginger Chicken (see page 134). It also works well in marinades for both meat and seafood, adding subtle depth to the final dish. Different brands of fish sauce vary considerably in flavor and saltiness, so it is worth experimenting to find one that appeals. As a good indication of quality, select a brand that specifically states anchovies (as opposed to simply fish) as its primary ingredient. If you can't find a Vietnamese sauce, Thai versions make a good substitute.

opposite: *ginger and galangal*

Five spice powder

The spicy sweetness of this aromatic powder fuses well with the balance of tastes required in Vietnamese cuisine. Although the actual ingredients vary, often comprising more than five spices, the core flavors are star anise, cloves, cinnamon (or cassia bark in more expensive brands), and fennel seed. Szechwan peppercorns, cardamom, and dried ginger might also be included in the mix. Being less intense than many spice mixes, five spice powder goes well with fish. Try lightly dusting a cod fillet before baking for a fragrant finish. The pungent sweetness also adds depth to marinades, such as that used for Crispy Quail with Watercress (see page 147).

Galangal

Galangal is a member of the ginger family. It bears a fairly close resemblance to ordinary ginger, though the paler galangal is distinguished by concentric rings, a more translucent skin, and a pink blush to its young tips. The taste, however, is unmistakable: less pungent but hot and peppery, with a bitter edge that makes ginger a poor substitute. Fresh galangal is available from speciality grocers and is preferred over the more strident powdered variety; if using the powder, add small amounts while monitoring the flavors carefully.

Ginger

A native of Southeast Asia, fresh ginger is used to season a broad variety of Vietnamese dishes. It is often added to the beef stock for pho bo, generally broiled or roasted first to bring out the flavors, and is a common ingredient of many other fish, chicken, or pork soups. Grated or finely sliced, ginger also features in marinades, grills, dipping sauces, and salads, providing a rich yet subtle, faintly woody aroma, while its fresh, sweet taste combines well with everything from seafood to stir-fried vegetables. Around Hue, a simple plate of scallops with ginger makes a popular dish.

Hoisin sauce

This thick, aromatic sauce made from soy beans blended with garlic, spices, and sugar is often referred to as Asia's barbecue sauce. Again, the combination of sweetness and spice lends itself naturally to the Vietnamese style of cooking. Heat hoisin with chile, rice vinegar, and lots of peanuts for a piquant, satay-like sauce (see page 54), perfect for dipping soft spring rolls or accompanying beef and seafood hot pots. It also adds flavor to Tamarind Sauce (see page 65) and can be used for a range of marinades. Hoisin sauce will keep for several months in the refrigerator.

opposite: *kaffir lime*

Jicama

Jicama, or yam bean, as it is also known, has a light crisp texture and a thin golden-beige skin. It is an ideal ingredient for livening up stir-fries and salads, more for its texture than flavor. To use in a salad, slice very thinly and dress in lime juice, then mix with slices of sour green mango. For stir-fries, chop in thin slivers and cook for a minute or less. Jicama makes a good substitute for water chestnuts as it has a similar bite and consistency.

Kaffir lime

There's nothing like the burst of citrus flavor you get from fresh kaffir lime leaves. Shredded very finely they make a wonderful addition to salads and can also be used like bay leaves to flavor soups and curries. Their lemon-lime tartness marries particularly well with coconut curries (see page 113), or try adding a leaf to the stock when making Fresh Soft Spring Rolls (see page 71). Be careful not to cook lime leaves too long, however, or they become bitter. Kaffir lime leaves are a dark and glossy green with a thick central rib (which should be removed before shredding) and a fragrant lemony aroma. The whole stem measures about four to six inches in length. Ideally, use either fresh or frozen leaves, which are available at specialty stores. Freeze-dried leaves, which you occasionally see in major supermarkets, are suitable for cooking but lack that lovely fresh bite required for salads or garnishes. Unfortunately, there is no particularly good substitute for lime leaves, though lemongrass would give some of the flavor. If you do find fresh leaves, place any surplus in a sealed container in the freezer where they will keep for up to six months. The fruit of the kaffir tree is used for Kaffir Lime Brûlée (see page 173). The fruit looks like a rather knobby lime and, again, is often stocked by Asian and Caribbean grocers. If kaffir limes are not available, use double the quantity of ordinary limes instead.

Lemongrass

Like the kaffir lime, lemongrass (or citronella) contributes a heady, lemon accent to many Southeast Asian dishes, notably soups and curries, though it also makes a dramatic dressing (see page 52). The grass has long, tapering, slightly bulbous stems, pale yellow in color, which release an intense lemon flavor when crushed. You can grow lemongrass quite easily as a house plant as long as it has sufficient sun. Otherwise, it is generally available either frozen or, preferably, fresh in Asian stores. Look for firm, unblemished stems and remove any damaged or wrinkled outer leaves before using. For dressings it's a good idea to remove the fibrous bulb before shredding the stem as finely as possible.

opposite & right: *sour green mango and sweet mango*

Lychees The white, semi-translucent flesh of the lychee, with its clean, slightly acid taste and firm texture, is a favorite ingredient for tropical fruit salads. Fresh lychees come into shops in late winter and spring, when they are easily identifiable by their knobbly, reddish brown skin – the redder it is, the riper the fruit. If desired, the hard seed can be removed by cutting the flesh in two and twisting it off the pit. Though fresh lychees are something of a luxury item, for Spiced Fruit Salad (see page 154) the canned variety serves just as well.

Mango Of the two varieties of mango used in the Bam-Bou kitchen, the sour green mango is the more difficult to source. It is smaller than the regular sweet mango, noticeably pointed at one end, and the skin is a brilliant shade of green. For Sour Green Mango Salad (see page 102) choose a hard, unripe fruit. Peel the outer skin carefully with a sharp knife or peeler, remove the big, flat pit from the center, and then shred the flesh into fine strips. Pale green and pleasantly sour, it provides a striking color contrast to the red of the chile and combines beautifully with the spicy sweetness of nuoc cham. If green mangoes are not available, drizzle freshly squeezed lime juice over unripened sweet mango as a substitute. The juicy, orange flesh of ripe sweet mango is superb on its own as a simple dessert or mixed into fruit salads. Stewed with mandarins and pickled ginger it also makes a lovely accompaniment to Sweet Coconut Rice (see page 157). The best test for ripeness is the fragrance, but the flesh should also give slightly to the touch while the skin of some varieties turns an orange-pink. Mangoes are often sold underripe; allow several days to ripen them at room temperature.

Mangosteen This relative of the lychee is a typical dessert fruit in Vietnam. Beneath a hard brown skin topped with four tiny petals is a fragrant, soft white flesh – one of the most succulent Southeast Asian fruits. Although they can be hard to find, mangosteens make an excellent addition to Spiced Fruit Salad (see page 154), but are also delicious eaten on their own or with ice cream for dessert.

opposite: *jicama, or yam bean*

Noodles Vietnamese noodles can be divided into three broad categories: noodles made with green mung bean flour, those made with rice flour, and Chinese-style egg noodles made from wheat flour. Most varieties for sale in the United States are dried. Mung bean noodles are known by several different names, of which bean thread vermicelli and glass or cellophane noodles are the most common. As implied, these noodles consist of very fine, almost translucent strands. They are much whiter and more crinkly than rice or egg noodles, and also harder. You need to soak them for five to ten minutes before cooking – but not too long or they will lose their crunchiness. Mung bean noodles are rarely served on their own. Instead, they are used primarily to give texture and structure to fillings. Crispy Spring Rolls (see page 74) is the classic example. Noodles made from rice flour come in a variety of shapes and sizes. The finest are generally known as rice vermicelli. These are slightly thicker and more opaque than mung bean noodles, and they have a much softer consistency when cooked. They make an ideal filling for Fresh Soft Spring Rolls (see page 71). To stop the cooked strands from sticking together, cool them rapidly under running water before sprinkling with a little sunflower oil. Slightly thicker rice noodles, comparable to spaghetti and referred to here as rice sticks, come into their own for more robust dishes such as soups and stir-fries. Broad flat rice noodles are an essential ingredient of Pho Bo (see page 68). Egg noodles are very yellow and round (roughly the diameter of spaghetti), and they have a nice nutty flavor.

Nuoc cham Nuoc cham is a milder, more palatable version of the fish sauce (see page 30) on which it is based. Its other essential ingredients are red chiles, garlic, and lemon juice, resulting in a thin, honey-colored liquid which is used for dressings, as a dipping sauce, and for marinades. Nuoc cham is best prepared a day or so in advance and left to infuse in the fridge – don't leave it too much longer or the chile will begin to dominate. To prevent the sauce from turning cloudy and bitter, wait until it is cold before adding the lemon juice. Like fish sauce, nuoc cham should enhance rather than overpower the accompanying flavors. This renders it extremely versatile and in Vietnam you will see it on every table, as a basic condiment and a dipping sauce. It also provides the foundation for a host of dressings. Add chopped fresh chile to nuoc cham for a piquant salad dressing, or mix it with equal quantities of lime to give a sour-sweet bite to a platter of Spicy Raw Beef (see page 131).

opposite: *mangosteen*

Oyster sauce

Made from oyster concentrate, sugar, and cornstarch cooked in brine, oyster sauce is widely used in southern China and Vietnam as a condiment, coloring agent, and flavoring. It is a rich brown color, thick, and salty sweet, carrying a hint of the sea rather than being markedly fishy. While this is another sauce that provides background flavor, a small quantity goes a long way, so start gently and adjust to taste, or tone it down with a little oil. It makes a good marinade for pork, but it also combines well with other meats. Alternatively, a dash or two will enhance a vegetable stir-fry. Oyster sauce is now stocked by most major supermarkets. In general, the more expensive, higher-quality brands have a more mellow flavor. Once opened, the sauce will keep, refrigerated, for two weeks, but canned varieties should be transferred to a jar to keep them from taking on an unpleasant metallic edge.

Pak choy

Chinese grocers, and most supermarkets these days, stock a wide variety of green-leafed Asian vegetables. Among them, pak choy is fairly easily identifiable as a cluster of broad, milky white stems with contrasting dark green, crinkly leaves. It is closely related to and largely interchangeable with bok choy (see page 29), though it has slightly more flavor, adding a peppery edge to dishes such as Wok-Seared Greens (see page 86). Again, it is important not to overcook pak choy. Young plants – anything from four to six inches long – will be most tender.

Papaya

A tropical fruit, papaya, or paw paw combines well with both sweet and savory dishes. There are dozens of different varieties, but in general it is a large, heavy fruit with a smooth, dusky green skin turning orange-red as it ripens. The ripe, semi-sweet flesh has a refreshing taste reminiscent of apricots and ginger, which makes a colorful addition to fruit salads, or it can be eaten on its own with a squeeze of lime to enhance the flavors. Choose a papaya that is still reasonably firm, split it open and remove the black seeds from the large central cavity, before dicing as required. Unripe, green papaya is less bulbous than the ripe variety and very hard, with a lighter green skin and a distinctive texture. As you peel and slice it, enzymes just beneath the skin leave a milky deposit on the knife. The flesh is very pale green and the seeds should still be white. Green papaya imparts little flavor but plenty of texture. It can also be used in crispy spring rolls or peeled and shredded into salads. If unavailable, replace with green unripe mango.

opposite: *pomegranates*

Pomegranate
Pomegranate fruits are the size of small oranges. Their tough outer skin turns from light brown to a rich purple-red as they ripen, as does the juicy, acid flesh packed with seeds. The fruit can be served fresh – simply slice across the top and use a spoon to scoop out the seeds, from which you suck off the flesh – or cooked in tarts, though it is best to split the seeds first.

Pomelo
Pomelos resemble large, thick-skinned grapefruits. The dry, semi-sweet flesh, which is occasionally pinkish red, is often used to provide contrasting flavor, texture, and color to savory dishes, such as Soft-Shell Crab With Mizuna (see page 105). Unripe grapefruit, or ripe grapefruit with a squeeze of lime juice, would be acceptable alternatives.

Rice vinegar
Less acidic and sweeter than white wine vinegar, rice vinegar features widely in Vietnamese cuisine. Its main use is in dipping sauces, marinades, and dressings, in which it provides a milder alternative to lime juice and tamarind, though still with a noticeably sharp edge. While rice vinegar generally serves as a background flavor, it can be mixed with generous amounts of lime juice and sugar to make a tangy dressing (see page 54) that would instantly lift a simple side dish of fresh bean sprouts or other salad greens.

Sake
Sake is a relatively strong, colorless Japanese wine made from fermented rice. Produced in both sweet and dry varieties, it can be used in cooking or as a drink to accompany the meal. Sake goes particularly well with fish. For the dishes at Bam-Bou, chef Mark favors a sweet sake with a slight acidity, which enhances other flavors. As a natural tenderizer, sake is excellent in marinades. Once the bottle is open it should be used within a week.

Sesame oil
The best sesame oil to use for Vietnamese cuisine is the blended form, where the oil's heady aroma and rich, nutty taste are toned down by the addition of soy or vegetable oil. To blend your own, dilute pure sesame oil with one third or one half the quantity of sunflower oil according to taste. Where a more intense flavor is required, as in Pan-Fried Duck Breast (see page 142), however, pure oil should be used. A dash of sesame oil enriches marinades and dressings.

opposite: *star fruit, or carambola*

Shiitake mushrooms

The delicious, oaky taste and earthy aroma of shiitake mushrooms are a common feature of Southeast Asian dishes. Sliced finely, fresh shiitake add body to stews, soups, and stir-fries. They are rarely eaten raw, however, since cooking really enhances the flavors. Choose firm, chestnut brown medium-sized caps, the thicker the better, with a pale brown underside. Before use, remove the woody stems and rinse. If fresh shiitake are not available, substitute with oyster mushrooms rather than ordinary button mushrooms, which lack the necessary texture and consistency. Dried shiitakes impart an intense smoky taste and have an even greater capacity to absorb flavors than the fresh mushroom. Again, look for meaty, medium-sized caps. Dried mushrooms are usually de-stemmed, but need to be soaked in hot water for five to ten minutes – save the strained water for soups and stocks. The finely sliced caps add texture to the filling for Crispy Spring Rolls (see page 74).

Soy sauce

Light soy sauce is preferred over dark in Vietnamese cooking because the latter imparts too much color. Light soy is also slightly thinner and milder, but can be substituted with dark soy by reducing the quantity used. The sauce's salty sweetness provides a subtle background to meat, seafood, or vegetable dishes, while just a few drops add a subtle finish sprinkled over rice or steamed fish.

Spring roll wrappers

At Bam-Bou, Mark uses two types of spring roll wrappers. For crispy spring rolls he buys ready-made square wrappers (8 by 8-inch) made from wheat flour, which are usually found in the freezer compartments of Asian grocers. Alternatively, a smaller size, or even the dried rounds described below, could be substituted. Unless using the whole packet, let the wrappers defrost at room temperature, peeling off the outer layers as they become pliable, before putting the remainder, still frozen, back in the freezer. Trim any ragged edges to get a neat square, then cover the wrappers with a damp cloth until you are ready to use them. The dried rice paper rounds used for soft spring rolls are sold as packets of translucent off-white crepes marked with a distinctive cross-hatch imprint from the bamboo drying frame. Mark recommends using medium-sized rice paper rounds, which are eight inches in diameter. In order to maintain the starchy finish, dip the rounds in hot water for ten to fifteen seconds, then fill and wrap them while they are still warm. Ideally, the rice paper should simply dissolve in the mouth.

opposite: *red chile*

Star fruit Sliced into fruit salads or combined with unripe banana, lettuce, and herbs as a side dish, there's no substitute for the pretty five-pointed star fruit, or carambola. Each fruit is about four to six inches long with a shiny yellow-green skin and pale yellow flesh when ripe. Firm, slightly unripe fruits are best to ensure the desired sweet-sour taste and crunchy texture. The only preparation required is to top and tail, then cut the fruit into thin cross-sections for a simple, attractive garnish.

Sugar cane Stalls selling foaming glasses of freshly crushed sugar cane juice are a common sight in Vietnam. Peeled and cut to size, the stems are also used as skewers, most often for grilling chao tom, Shrimp on Sugar Cane (see page 120). Both fresh and canned cane are available in Asian or Caribbean stores. Though it is more expensive and difficult to prepare, fresh cane provides a lovely burst of fresh sugar flavor as you bite through the shrimp-meat wrapping. First, remove the skin by cutting down towards the table with a sharp knife, then divide the peeled cane into four-inch lengths between the hard knuckles; a serrated knife will make this easier. Split the sections lengthways into quarters before trimming them down to the required size. Longer lengths of canned cane, preserved in syrup, may need to be halved before splitting into batons. It is worth mentioning that the sugar cane is not supposed to be eaten – just bite on it gently to release the sweetness.

Sweet chile sauce Red chiles, garlic, sugar, and vinegar combined create a thick, hot, and sweet orange-red sauce which appears on restaurant tables throughout Southeast Asia. Bottled sweet chile sauce, available in supermarkets, may be smooth or contain seeds – the choice is a matter of individual preference. Once opened, it will keep for several months stored in a cool, dark place.

Sweet soy sauce Dark, syrupy, and highly aromatic, this caramelized soy sauce is usually marketed under its Indonesian name, kecap (or kejap) manis. In Indonesia it is a popular dipping sauce for satay, while Mark uses it here to add a lovely smoky flavor to dishes such as Crispy Quail with Watercress (see page 147). Unlike ordinary soy, it is also a good coating sauce. Broiled Chicken Brochettes (see page 76), for example, are bathed in sweet soy sauce before broiling to produce a lovely, rich brown glaze.

opposite: *sugar cane*

Tamarind

Long, plump, and bean-like, the ripe pods of the tamarind tree have brittle chocolate-brown shells that crack open like a peanut to reveal a thick, fibrous brown pulp protecting the seeds. This pulp is extracted and used as a sour-sweet flavoring. It is most commonly on sale in specialty grocers as blocks of compressed pulp, still containing the seeds, or in a more convenient puréed form. If using the pulp, cut it into small pieces and leave it to stew for about an hour to extract the flavors, then strain to remove the large black seeds and fibers. The resulting liquid has a clean, tart taste, which you may want to use sparingly to start with but which can really lift the flavor of dishes. Any leftover pulp keeps well stored in an airtight container.

Tofu

Tofu, or soybean curd, is the ideal base ingredient: inexpensive, packed with protein, low in calories, and easy to digest. It is also extremely versatile and, though considered bland, readily soaks up flavors to blend into almost any dish. Soft (silken) tofu tends to disintegrate on cooking, so choose either firm or semi-firm tofu for the fried eggplant dish (see page 90). Even so, you might like to flake a little extra on top as a garnish just before serving so that the crispiness of the eggplant contrasts with the softness of the tofu and tomatoes. Most supermarkets nowadays stock fresh tofu sealed in water-filled containers. Though best used within a day of purchase, it will keep for up to a week in the fridge as long as it is immersed in fresh water and the water is changed daily.

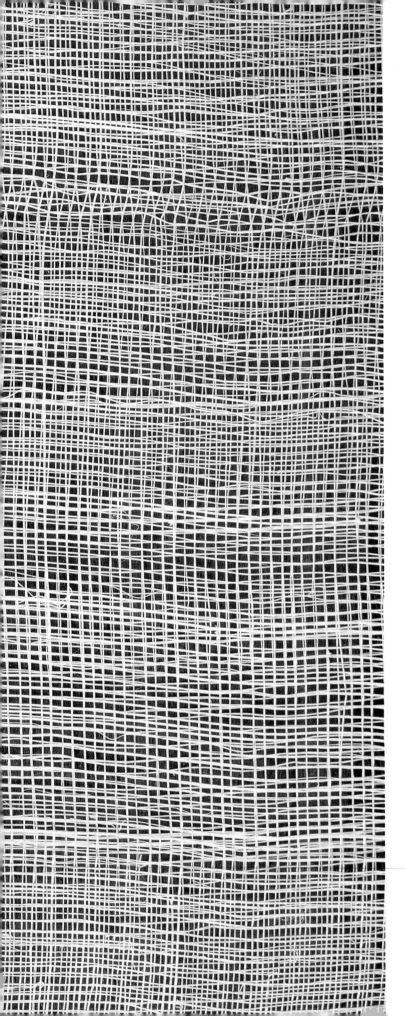

basics

"The market is full of odors which leap in to your face and your heart, and make you turn your head: cinammon, saffron with here and there a hint of pepper or ginger."

Vietnamiennes au Quotidien, Francoise Corrèze, 1982

lemongrass dressing

1 Strain the nuoc cham through a fine sieve into a bowl to remove the garlic and chiles.

2 Slice the lemongrass as finely as possible.

3 Mix all the ingredients together in a bowl and leave covered in the refrigerator for at least 6 hours before serving to allow all the flavors to infuse.

 To get the maximum amount of juice from a lemon, roll it back and forth on a hard surface a few times, exerting pressure from the palm of your hand, prior to juicing. Alternatively, cut the lemon in half, then insert a fork and twist the flesh back and forth a few times first.

Lemongrass Dressing is ideal served with Grilled Chicken Brochettes with Lemongrass Noodles (see page 76). It will keep, covered, in the refrigerator for up to two weeks.

ingredients 125ml/4fl oz Nuoc Cham (see page 57) | 2 sticks of lemongrass | 6 tablespoons sake | 4 tablespoons lemon juice (about 2 lemons)

lime & rice wine vinegar dressing

1   Cut the limes in half and use a juicer to extract all the juice. Discard any seeds.

2   In a bowl, combine the lime juice with the remaining dressing ingredients. Stir to allow the sugar and salt to dissolve, about 2 minutes.

This dressing could be served with raw bean sprouts or Spicy Herbed Leaf Salad (see page 93). To extract the maximum amount of juice from the limes, use the same rolling technique that you use for lemons (see page 52). Store, covered, in the refrigerator for up to two weeks.

ingredients 6 limes | 150ml/¼ pint rice vinegar | 3 tablespoons superfine sugar | 1 tablespoon salt

peanut & hoisin sauce

1   In a small heavy-based saucepan over low heat, warm the water, vinegar, and peanut butter until blended, stirring occasionally.

2   Stir in the hoisin and hot chile sauces.

3   Finish off by stirring in the chopped peanuts.

Chile sauce adds to the flavor of this dipping sauce. It is a perfect accompaniment to Fresh Soft Spring Roll with Chicken, Rice Noodles, Mint & Cilantro or Vietnamese Hot Pot with Beef, Prawns & Squid (see pages 71 and 79). Store, covered, in the refrigerator for up to two weeks.

ingredients 4 tablespoons water | 4 tablespoons rice vinegar | 7 tablespoons crunchy peanut butter | 8 tablespoons hoisin sauce | 1 tablespoon hot chile sauce | 1 tablespoon unsalted peanuts, roasted and finely chopped

bitter lemon dressing

1   Use a sharp knife to carefully remove the rind from the limes and lemons. Juice the fruit and discard the seeds.

2   Wash the mint and set aside to drain.

3   In a large heavy-based saucepan, warm the juice of the fresh fruit and the bitter lemon juice together. Do not allow the mixture to boil.

4   Stir in the sugar, remove from the heat and continue stirring until the sugar has dissolved. Leave to cool.

5   To serve, finely shred the mint leaves and add to the cooled dressing.

Make this dressing at least one day in advance to allow the mint to infuse. Serve with dishes such as Crispy Marinated Squid with Bitter Lemon Dressing, Crispy Spring Roll with Prawns, Crispy Smoked Chicken with Fragrant Greens, , Pork & Mushrooms and Muc Nhoi Stuffed Squid (see pages 74, 101, 128, and 124). Store, covered, in the refrigerator for up to two weeks.

ingredients 2 limes | 3 lemons | 1 bunch of mint, freshly picked (if possible) | 250ml/8fl oz bottled bitter lemon juice | 50g/2oz superfine sugar

nuoc cham (dipping sauce)

1 Peel and finely chop the garlic. Slice the chiles in
   half, deseed, and finely chop.

2 In a large heavy-based saucepan, warm (do not boil)
   the fish sauce, water, vinegar, sugar, garlic, and
   chiles. When the sauce becomes moderately hot,
   (about 60°C/140°F), remove the saucepan from
   the heat and allow to cool.

3 When the sauce has completely cooled, stir in the
   lemon juice.

*To turn this recipe into a vegetarian
dipping sauce, replace the fish sauce with
30ml/1fl oz light soy sauce. The chiles and garlic
can be increased or decreased to your desired taste.
The dipping sauce will keep for at least one week,
covered, in the refrigerator, and should be made at
least a day in advance of use to allow the flavors of
the chiles and garlic to infuse.*

ingredients 5 garlic cloves ❙ 5 large red chiles ❙ 50ml/2fl oz fish sauce ❙ 100ml/3½fl oz water ❙ 50ml/2fl oz rice
vinegar ❙ 50g/2oz superfine sugar ❙ 50ml/2fl oz freshly squeezed lemon juice (about 1 large lemon)

galangal sauce

1   Peel and finely chop the shallots. Peel, wash, and chop the galangal and ginger, including the peelings. Place in a large heavy-based saucepan and sauté without allowing to color, stirring occasionally, for about 3 minutes.

2   In another saucepan, melt the butter and add the flour to make a roux. Slowly cook over low heat until the texture becomes sandy, about 2 minutes.

3   Pour the fish stock into the pan with the sauté mixture. Reduce, stirring, over a medium heat to allow the flavor of the galangal and ginger to come through, about 15 minutes. Add the stock to the roux, stirring continuously to prevent it from catching and burning. To add a little extra flavor, stir in the cilantro stalks.

4   Season and stir in the cream. Return to a boil, then pass through a large fine sieve. Push the vegetables through firmly with a metal spoon to extract as much flavor as possible. Shred the cilantro leaves and stir them into the sauce.

ingredients   3 large shallots | 2 stems galangal | 1 small piece of fresh ginger | 15g/½oz unsalted butter |
3 teaspoons flour | 1 liter/1¾ pints Fish Stock (see page 63) | 1 bunch of cilantro, freshly picked (if possible) |
1 teaspoon each: salt and freshly ground black pepper | 250ml/8fl oz heavy cream

ginger dressing

1 Peel and finely dice the garlic and ginger.

2 Slice the chile in half lengthwise, then deseed and finely dice.

3 Slice the limes in half, remove the seeds, and extract all the juice with a juicer.

4 Place the fish sauce, ginger, garlic, and chile into a large heavy-based saucepan. Heat until hot to the touch, around 60°C/140°F). (Do not boil the liquid; you just want to take out the bite out of the ginger.)

5 Allow the dressing to cool completely, then stir in the lime juice.

 Avoid blending the ginger, garlic, and chile together as this will take a lot of the flavor out of the dressing and it will also absorb the juice.

This dressing can be served with Pan-Fried Duck Breast with Crispy Greens & Sesame Soy Dressing (see page 142). It is also a good alternative dipping sauce for Crispy Spring Roll with Prawns, Pork & Mushrooms, or Muc Nhoi Stuffed Squid (see pages 74 and 124). When served as a dipping sauce, it is better made a day in advance to allow the flavors to infuse. Store, covered, in the refrigerator for up to one week .

ingredients 2 garlic cloves **|** 1 large piece of freh ginger **|** 1 red chile **|** 2 limes **|** 6 tablespoons fish sauce

sticky rice

1   In a large bowl, soak the rice in 500ml/17fl oz cold water for 10 minutes. Strain and rinse through cold running water to remove the excess starch.

2   Fill a large heavy-based pot one quarter full with water. Have a smaller pot (one that will fit inside the larger one) ready with the rice and the remaining water. Alternatively, see note below.

3   Bring the water in the larger pot to a boil and then place the smaller one carefully inside. Cover with either plastic wrap or a lid.

4   Reduce the heat and leave the rice to simmer for about 10 minutes, stirring occasionally, until cooked and sticky. The rice is now ready to serve.

 A proper rice steamer is an expensive addition to your kitchen, but the same result can be achieved in a bain-marie at very little cost. Once you have mastered the basic technique, cooking Sticky Rice will become very easy and it will be second nature to serve it with any number of dishes featured in this book.

ingredients 300g/10oz glutinous rice | 750ml/1¼ pints water

pho bo veal stock

1 Preheat oven to 220°C (425°F) Gas Mark 7. In a roasting pan, roast the veal bones for about 2 hours until brown. Transfer to a large saucepan or casserole.

2 Heat some oil in the same roasting pan and fry the prepared garlic and vegetables until brown, about 6–8 minutes. Stir in the tomato purée and canned tomatoes. Add the bay leaves and leave the mixture to thicken, stirring occasionally, about 4 minutes. Add salt and pepper.

3 Pour the prepared vegetable mixture over the veal bones. Fill to the top with cold water. Bring the stock to a boil, stirring. Skim away the excess fat and reduce the heat to simmering point.

4 Leave the stock to simmer away for about 3 hours, skimming and stirring as necessary. Pass through a large fine sieve into a bowl. Leave to cool completely and to become slightly jellied in appearance.

5 For the clarification mix, peel, wash, and cut the carrot, onion, leek, and celery into small pieces. Place in the bowl of a food processor, together with the peeled garlic and prepared lemongrass. Pulse until minced.

6 Fold in the egg whites and stir the peppercorns into the mixture.

7 Remove any fat from the prepared stock and fold in the clarification mix.

8 Return the saucepan or casserole to the heat and bring to a boil, stirring. Once boiled, reduce the heat to low and leave until a crust has formed. (At this stage do not touch the stock or it will begin to cloud.) Cut a small section away to see the clarification process take place. Simmer slowly for about 1 hour.

9 Remove the stock from the heat and pass through a fine cloth or a large fine sieve into a bowl, taking care not to disturb the crust.

ingredients 2.5kg/5lb veal bones ▌ a little vegetable or sunflower oil for frying ▌ 3 garlic cloves, peeled and roughly chopped ▌ 1 large carrot, onion, and leek, roughly chopped ▌ 1 stick of celery, roughly chopped ▌ 2 tablespoons tomato purée ▌ 300g/10oz canned tomatoes, chopped ▌ 4 bay leaves, freshly picked (if possible) ▌ 6 liters/10½ pints water ▌ salt and freshly ground black pepper ▌ FOR THE CLARIFICATION 1 carrot ▌ 1 onion ▌ 1 leek ▌ 1 stick of celery ▌ 2 garlic cloves ▌ 3 sticks of lemongrass, roughly chopped ▌ 300g/10oz egg whites (the egg whites from about 10 eggs) ▌ 1 tablespoon black peppercorns

fish stock

1 Wash, peel, and cut the vegetables roughly into small pieces.

2 Melt some butter in a large heavy-based saucepan and sweat the vegetables for about 6 minutes. (Do not allow the vegetables to color.)

3 Add the fish bones and fry for a few minutes. Pour in the cold water and add the lemongrass, ginger, peppercorns, and salt. Stir the stock and bring to a boil. As soon as it begins to boil, skim the surface (do not stir or the stock will become cloudy) and reduce the heat to simmering point.

4 Leave the stock to simmer for 1 hour, then pass through a large fine sieve into a bowl.

The stock can be stored, covered, in the refrigerator, for up to one week and makes 750ml/1¼ pints, which is enough for four people. It is used to make Galangal Sauce (see page 58).

ingredients 1 stick of celery ❘ 1 leek ❘ 1 large onion ❘ a little butter for frying ❘ 600g/1lb 5oz white fish bones ❘ 2liters/3½ pints water ❘ 2 sticks of lemongrass ❘ 1 stem of ginger ❘ 2 tablespoons whole black peppercorns ❘ 1 teaspoon salt

chicken stock

1   Remove the fat from the chicken carcasses or
    wings and rinse them under cold running water.

2   Wash, peel, and roughly dice the vegetables.

3   In a large heavy-based saucepan, melt some butter
    and fry the vegetables without coloring, about 6
    minutes.

4   Add the carcasses and remaining ingredients.
    Fill to the top with cold water.

5   Bring the stock to a boil, skim the surface,
    then reduce the heat to simmering point. Leave to
    simmer for 1 hour, skimming occasionally.

6   Pass the stock through a fine sieve into a large bowl.
    Allow to cool before removing any excess fat.
    Cover and refrigerate until needed.

Although more expensive, chicken wings work well in this recipe. When cooled and refrigerated properly, this stock can be made a few days in advance of use. It can be stored, covered, in the refrigerator for up to one week and makes 750ml/1¼ pints, which is enough for four people.

ingredients 1kg/2lb chicken carcasses or wings ▌ 1 onion ▌ 1 leek ▌ 1 stick of celery ▌ a little butter, for frying ▌ 2 liters/3½ pints water ▌ 2 bay leaves, freshly picked (if possible) ▌ 2 garlic cloves ▌ 1 bunch of cilantro, freshly picked (if possible) ▌ 1 teaspoon coriander seeds ▌ 1 teaspoon whole black peppercorns

tamarind sauce

1 Plunge the tomatoes into a heatproof bowl full of boiling water. Leave for 10 seconds. Use a slotted spoon to lift them out of the bowl and remove the skins with a sharp knife. Cut the tomatoes into halves, deseed, and finely chop.

2 Peel and finely slice the garlic cloves.

3 Chop the tamarind paste into small pieces.

4 Place the remaining ingredients in a large heavy-based saucepan. Leave to simmer for about 1 hour, stirring occasionally.

5 Blend the sauce while it is still warm in a food processor and pass through a large fine sieve into a bowl to obtain as much sauce as possible.

This sauce is ideal served with Five-Spiced Cod with Tamarind & Herbs (see page 119). Store, covered, in the refrigerator for up to one week.

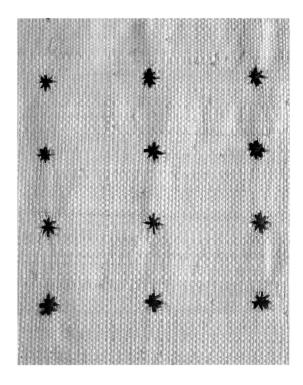

ingredients 250g/8oz plum tomatoes **|** 3 garlic cloves **|** 250g/8oz tamarind pulp **|** 250ml/8fl oz pineapple juice **|** 400ml/14fl oz water **|** 1 cinnamon stick **|** 3 tablespoons hoisin sauce **|** 6 tablespoons superfine sugar **|** 120ml/4fl oz sweet soy sauce

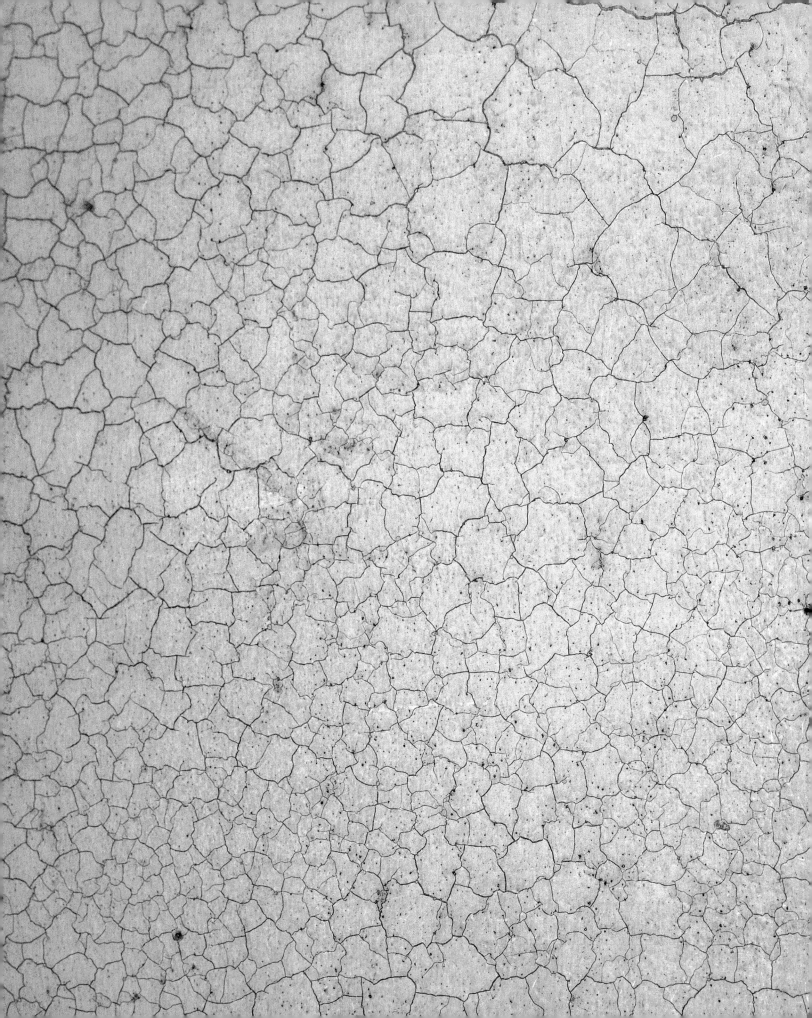

noodles & rice

"The educated man preceeds the farmer.

But when the rice begins to run short, it is

the farmer who comes first."

Old Vietnamese Saying

pho bo beef & noodle soup

1   Bring a large heavy-based saucepan of salted water (enough to cover the noodles) to a boil. Blanch the noodles, about 3 minutes. (Do not overcook at this stage as they will be cooked again later.)

2   Meanwhile, mix together all the ingredients for the garnish in a small bowl.

3   In another saucepan, bring the stock to a boil, whisk in the hoisin sauce and season to taste.

4   Divide the noodles between 4 soup bowls and divide half the garnish between the bowls. Pour the stock over the garnish.

5   Place the beef slices on top of the garnish so that they do not sink into the soup. Slice the limes in half and squeeze the juice of half a lime over each portion of beef.

6   To serve, place the remaining garnish in a bowl so that your guests can help themselves if they wish. Serve the soup with the remaining lime halves. Have your guests mix their own soup together as this process cooks the beef.

As an alternative to serving this dish with the usual condiments of salt and pepper, try making up a batch of spiced salt, which will also go with just about any other dish. In a food processor or blender, grind 250g (8oz) of rock salt with 1 dried red chile and 20g (³/₄oz) of Farchiew, or Szechuan, spice (or substitute dried pink peppercorns). Serve alongside the soup in a small bowl.

ingredients   600g/1¼ lb flat rice noodles, | 1 liter/1¾ pints Pho Bo Veal Stock (see page 62) | 4 tablespoons hoisin sauce | 200g/7oz raw beef striploin, French cut, trimmed of fat, and finely sliced | 4 limes | salt and freshly ground black pepper | FOR THE GARNISH   160g/5½oz fresh bean sprouts | 4 sprigs each: cilantro and Asian basil freshly picked (if possible) and roughly chopped | 2 red chiles, finely sliced and deseeded

vegetable & peanut noodle stir-fry

1 Bring a large heavy-based saucepan of boiling salted water to a boil and blanch the noodles for 2 minutes. Refresh in cold water and set aside.

2 Wash and peel the carrots, slice them in half, and cut into very thin sticks. Wash and shred the leek in the same way.

3 Rinse and cut the peppers in half; deseed and cut into sticks in the same way as the carrots and leek.

5 Peel the shallots lengthwise and slice as finely as possible.

5 In a dry, heavy-based frying pan, toast the peanuts until brown, about 4–5 minutes. Chop and reserve.

6 Wash, top and tail, then shred the spring onions.

7 Heat some oil in a wok and when hot, add the carrots, leeks, peppers, and shallots. Fry, stirring occasionally, for about 2 minutes.

8 Refresh the noodles in boiling salted water for a few seconds. Drain thoroughly and add to the wok. Stir to mix all the ingredients in the wok together, then stir in the hoisin peanut sauce and add the spring onion. Fry for about 2 minutes, stirring.

9 To serve, arrange the contents of the wok on a serving platter and top with chopped peanuts.

Peanuts give this dish a very distinctive flavor. For a non-peanut version, Tamarind Sauce (see page 65), although very sweet, would also work in place of the Peanut & Hoisin sauce. This dish can be served as a main course or as an accompaniment to Grilled Chicken Brochettes with Lemongrass Noodles or Barbecued Pork Ribs with Hoisin (see pages 76 and 144).

ingredients 200g/7oz rice stick noodles ▮ 2 large carrots ▮ 1 large leek ▮ 1 red pepper ▮ 1 green pepper ▮ 3 shallots ▮ 4 tablespoons unsalted peanuts ▮ 2 bunches of spring onions ▮ a little sunflower or vegetable oil for frying ▮ 6 tablespoons Peanut & Hoisin Sauce (see page 54)

fresh soft spring roll with chicken, rice noodles, mint & cilantro

1 Place the lettuce leaves on a work surface. Pile the filling ingredients into each one, starting and finishing with the sliced chicken. (Allow 3 mint and 3 cilantro leaves per roll.)

2 Roll each of the lettuce leaves into a tight bundle to form a cylindrical shape and trim away the excess lettuce. (There should be enough lettuce to wrap round the mixture once.)

3 Fill a large heatproof bowl with hot water and dip the rice paper sheets individually into the water until they become soft and sticky, about 15 seconds. While warm, lay them out flat on damp cloths.

4 Place a lettuce roll slightly off center on top of each rice paper sheet. Aiming to keep the roll tight, fold the two sides of the rolls over into the center. Roll as tightly as possible with your hands. As you complete each roll, keep it wrapped in a damp cloth.

5 To serve, unwrap the rolls from the damp cloth and leave to warm slightly next to the stove. Cut each roll across the center at a slight angle and serve with 2 sprigs each of cilantro and mint and small dipping bowls of Nuoc Cham.

 This recipe would be ideal served as a starter dish.

ingredients 8 iceberg lettuce leaves, rinsed | 8 sheets of rice paper for wrapping | 8 sprigs each: mint and cilantro, freshly picked (if possible) for the garnish | Nuoc Cham, for dipping (see page 57) | FOR THE SOFT ROLL FILLING 2 chicken breasts, poached in Chicken Stock and sliced (see page 64) | 80g/3¼oz rice vermicelli noodles, cooked until soft (follow the directions on the packet), then chopped into segments | 1 carrot and 1 cucumber, peeled and cut into julienne strips | 40g/1½oz fresh bean sprouts | 24 leaves each: mint and cilantro, freshly picked (if possible)

fresh soft spring roll with chicken, rice noodles, mint & cilantro

(recipe on previous page)

crispy spring roll with prawns, pork & mushrooms

1 To make the spring roll filling, peel and finely chop the shallot. Slice the chile in half; deseed and finely dice.

2 Peel and finely chop the garlic, then peel and grate the carrot. Combine the shallot, chile, garlic, carrot, and bean sprouts together in a large bowl.

3 Soak both types of mushroom in a bowl of warm water for 5 minutes, squeeze dry, and finely slice.

4 Now soak the noodles in cold water for 5 minutes. Drain and cut the noodles and mushrooms into small pieces and mix together with the pork mince and the ingredients in the bowl.

5 Cut the prawn tails into small pieces.

6 To make up the rolls one at a time, open one spring roll wrapper and angle it so that the corner point is facing you. Spoon about 4 teaspoons of the filling mixture just slightly off center (towards you) in a cigar shape, then place a small amount of chopped prawns (about 2 teaspoons) on top (allow enough room to fold the wrapper in at the sides).

7 Lightly brush all the way around the edge of the wrapper with the egg white.

8 Fold the point of the wrapper nearest to you over the mix and seal it tightly. Now fold in both sides to give the length of the completed roll. Finally, pressing quite tightly, roll up the wrapper to form the roll. Lay on a flat surface with the final point of the wrapper facing down so that the egg can stick. Repeat to make eight rolls (two per person).

9 Rinse the lettuce and herbs on the stems (ensure that they are fresh and crispy as the idea is to wrap the finished rolls with lettuce and herbs as you eat them).

10 Heat some oil in a deep-fat fryer until hot. Deep fry the rolls for about 2 minutes, or until cooked through and crispy all over.

11 To serve, either cut the spring rolls in half or serve them whole on top of a lettuce leaf on individual plates. Serve with a sprig of each herb and a little dipping pot of Nuoc Cham.

ingredients 8 sheets spring roll wrappers (8⅔ by 8⅔ inches) **|** 3 egg whites **|** 8 iceberg lettuce leaves **|** 4 sprigs each: mint and cilantro, freshly picked (if possible) **|** a little sunflower or vegetable oil for deep frying **|** 120ml/4fl oz Nuoc Cham (see page 57) **|** FOR THE SPRING ROLL FILLING 1 large shallot **|** 1 red chile **|** 1 garlic clove **|** 1 carrot **|** 50g/2oz bean sprouts **|** 1 large dried black fungus mushroom **|** 2 dried shiitake mushrooms **|** 50g/2oz bean thread vermicelli noodles **|** 200g/7oz minced pork (or minced chicken for a slightly softer mixture) **|** 125g/4oz raw prawn tails, meat only, no shell and deveined (your fishmonger can do this for you)

broiled chicken brochettes with lemongrass noodles

1   Cut each chicken thigh in half lengthwise to allow
    for three skewers per person.

2   To make the marinade, finely chop the lemongrass,
    then peel and finely chop the garlic. Place them
    in a large shallow bowl and mix in the sauces and
    caramel. Add the chicken and stir gently to coat
    it with the sauce. Leave to marinate, covered, for
    4 hours in the refrigerator.

3   Meanwhile, to make the dressing, finely slice the
    lemongrass and place it in a large bowl. Stir in the
    lemon juice, sake, and Nuoc Cham. Leave to infuse,
    covered, for 4 hours in the refrigerator.

4   Bring a large heavy-based saucepan of boiling salted
    water to a boil and cook the rice noodles according
    to the packet directions until soft
    (just slightly undercooked). This will lend a melting
    texture to the noodles in the final dish.

5   In a dry heavy-based frying pan, toast the peanuts.
    Leave to cool, then transfer to a plastic bag. Seal the
    bag and crush the peanuts into small pieces with a
    rolling pin.

6   Soak the bamboo skewers in cold water for a few
    minutes to soften them. Skewer the chicken pieces
    lengthwise, threading them gently through the
    skewers and spreading them out as you go.
    (Remember to leave some space at the end of the
    skewers so that they can be held.)

7   If available, cook on a grill, turning occasionally
    until just underdone, about 2 minutes. Alternatively,
    broil for about 3 minutes, turning halfway through.

8   Coat the brochettes with the sweet soy sauce and
    return to the grill or broiler until the soy sauce has
    thickened and the chicken is thoroughly coated,
    about 1 minute each side.

9   Marinate the noodles in a little of the dressing for
    about 1 minute.

10 To serve, arrange the marinated noodles around
    each plate as desired. Place the skewered chicken on
    top and sprinkle with peanuts. Serve the remaining
    dressing in individual dipping bowls.

ingredients 6 chicken thighs, skinned and boned (your butcher can do this for you) ▌ 125g/4oz rice vermicelli
noodles ▌ 4 tablespoons unsalted peanuts (optional) ▌ 12 bamboo skewers ▌ 60ml/4 tablespoons sweet soy sauce ▌
FOR THE MARINADE 2 sticks of lemongrass ▌ 1 garlic clove ▌ 4 tablespoons light soy sauce ▌ 2 tablespoons fish sauce ▌
3 tablespoons caramel (see Sesame Banana Fritters, page 162) ▌ FOR THE DRESSING 1 stick of lemongrass ▌ juice of 2 lemons
▌ 4 tablespoons sake ▌ 6 tablespoons Nuoc Cham (see page 57)

Vietnamese hot pot with beef, prawns & squid

1 Cut the steak and chicken into small strips and cut the prawns in half lengthwise.

2 Next, cut the squid from the tail to the tip (to end up with one flat piece of squid). Lay each piece inside out and clean all the sinews. Slightly score by cutting through two-thirds of the flesh in a criss-cross design, then cut into strips.

3 Peel the carrots and cut in half; thinly slice lengthwise. Wipe and thinly slice the mushrooms and peel and thinly slice the shallots.

4 Trim the celery (reserving the leaves as a garnish) and slice into thin strips.

5 Wash the cilantro and watercress, including the stalks, and wash the bok choy. Leave to drain, roughly chop, and set aside.

6 Slice the chiles in half lengthwise, deseed, and chop into small pieces. Leave to soak in cold water for 10 minutes. Meanwhile, blanch the noodles in a large heavy-based saucepan of boiling salted water for about 3 minutes until soft. Drain, leave to cool and set aside in a bowl of cold water.

7 In a large heavy-based saucepan, bring the stock to a boil. Add the mushrooms, carrots, celery, shallots, chiles and bok choy. Return to a boil, add the steak, chicken, prawns, and squid and cook for 2-3 minutes.

8 To serve, add the drained noodles and return the hot pot to a boil. Stir in the cilantro, reserved celery leaves, and watercress and serve immediately.

Serve with Stir-Fried Ginger Noodles or Wok-Seared Greens (see pages 83 and 86). You could also serve the hot pot with a small bowl of spiced salt (see page 68).

ingredients 100g/3½oz sirloin steak, fat-free | 100g/3½oz chicken breast, fat-free | 100g/3½oz raw prawn tails, deveined if available (your fishmonger can do this for you) | 100g/3½oz squid bodies and tentacles (weight is when cleaned) | 2 large carrots | 100g/3½oz shiitake mushrooms | 2 large shallots | 2 sticks of celery, leafy (if possible) | 8 cilantro sprigs, freshly picked (if possible) | 1 bunch of watercress | 2 heads of bok choy | 4 dried chiles | 200g/7oz rice stick noodles | 1 liter/1¾ pints Chicken Stock (see page 64)

spicy noodle salad

1   Rinse and peel the carrot and cucumber. Cut the cucumber in half lengthwise, deseed, and cut both the carrots and cucumber into julienne, or matchstick, strips.

2   Peel and cut the shallots lengthwise, then finely slice.

3   Rinse the bean sprouts. Slice the chiles in half lengthwise, deseed, and finely slice to create rings of chile. Reserve a small amount for the garnish.

4   Bring a large heavy-based saucepan of salted water to a boil and cook the noodles until just underdone, about 2 minutes. Refresh under cold water and drain. Set aside.

5   Shred the cilantro and mint.

6   In a large mixing bowl, place all the ingredients apart from the herbs and including the Nuoc Cham; thoroughly combine.

7   To serve, place the salad in a serving bowl and finish off with a sprinkling of fresh herbs and the reserved chiles.

For a vegetarian option, exchange the Nuoc Cham for the vegetarian version (see page 57). This dish makes a good starter, accompaniment or just a snack. The amount of chile can be changed according to taste but bear in mind that this is meant to be a spicy dish.

This dish complements Grilled Fillet of Lemon Sole Wrapped in Banana Leaves, Cha-Ca Monkfish with Turmeric, Dill & Onion, and Farchiew Pork Fillet (see pages 109, 110, and 132), to name but a few.

ingredients 1 medium carrot | 1 cucumber | 2 shallots | 50g/2oz bean sprouts | 3 red chiles | 200g/7oz rice vermicelli noodles | 6 tablespoons Nuoc Cham (see page 57) | FOR THE GARNISH 1 small bunch each: cilantro and mint, freshly picked (if possible)

stir-fried ginger noodles

1   Bring a large heavy-based saucepan of salted water to a boil and blanch the noodles for about 2 minutes. Refresh under cold water.

2   Peel and finely chop the ginger and garlic.

3   Cut the chile in half lengthwise, deseed, and finely chop.

4   Shred the spring onions and pick the leaves from the cilantro. Wipe and slice the shiitake mushrooms.

5   Heat the sunflower oil in a large heavy-based wok. When hot, fry the garlic, ginger, chile, and mushrooms until brown, about 3 minutes. Add the noodles and spring onion; stir to combine, about 3 minutes.

6   To serve, arrange the noodles in a serving dish and garnish with cilantro leaves.

 This dish can be served as either a starter, snack, or accompaniment. You can reduce or even increase the amount of chiles according to taste. It goes perfectly with Cha-Ca Monkfish with Turmeric, Dill & Onion, Curried Frog's Legs, or Crispy Quail with Watercress (see pages 110, 123, and 147), to name but a few.

ingredients 200g/7oz egg noodles **|** 1 large piece of fresh ginger **|** 2 garlic cloves **|** 1 large red chile **|** 4 spring onions **|** 100g/3¾oz shiitake mushrooms **|** 4 tablespoons sunflower oil **|** FOR THE GARNISH 2 sprigs cilantro, freshly picked

vegetables & salads

"The green coconut palm with its great plume

of leaves stretches its arms to welcome the

breeze and signals to the moon."

Tran Dong Khoa, 1967

wok-seared greens

1 Fill a large heavy-based saucepan with salted water and bring to a boil. Meanwhile, top and tail the beans, then blanch for 1 minute. Remove with a slotted spoon and set aside.

2 Trim the broccoli and blanch in the water for 2 minutes. Remove with a slotted spoon and set aside.

3 Pick the leaves from the spinach. Wash and rewash if still gritty. Drain thoroughly on paper towels.

4 Pick the leaves from the stems of the pak choy and bok choy; wash and drain as in step 3.

5 Heat a large heavy-based wok until hot. Add a drizzle of oil and, once hot, quickly add the greens and toss them in the oil. Add the broccoli and beans; toss, then add the spinach, seasoning, and soy sauce. Toss to combine all the ingredients and serve immediately.

This seared vegetable dish should be served crunchy and well seasoned. The vegetables listed above are the ones most commonly used but they can be substituted as desired. However, avoid substituting alternatives for pak choy and bok choy as they lend a distinctive flavor to the recipe. Be careful when adding the vegetables to the hot wok. They will flame if the pan is too hot.

ingredients 125g/4oz green beans | 2 heads of broccoli | 2 handfuls of spinach leaves | 2 heads each: pak choy and bok choy | a little sunflower oil for frying | 120ml/4fl oz light soy sauce | salt and freshly ground black pepper

spinach & mushroom pancakes

1   To make the pancake batter, finely chop the spinach and purée in a blender or food processor.

2   In a large bowl, whisk together the milk and egg. Sift in the flour and whisk it into the mixture, then add the spinach purée and season.

3   Over high heat, melt a pat of butter in a medium heavy-based nonstick frying pan. Swirl the butter round to cover the pan. Reduce the heat to medium.

4   Add about 2 tablespoons of batter to the pan and tip the pan from side to side so that it is evenly coated with batter. The pancake will take about half a minute to cook. Lift the edge with a spatula (it should be light golden in color). There is no need to turn it over as it will be cooked through.

5   Remove the pancake and allow to cool on a rack. Repeat to make 8 pancakes. Stack the pancakes together, cover with plastic wrap and refrigerate.

6   For the filling, finely shred the spring onions, wipe and slice the mushrooms finely, and then finely chop the spinach.

7   Heat a wok and, when hot, add the sunflower oil. Fry the onions and mushrooms over high heat. Reduce the heat and stir in the spinach; season. Stir in the sauces and allow to cool.

8   Prior to serving remove the pancakes from the refrigerator. Divide the filling between each pancake and roll them up.

9   Make the tomato sauce. As a variation, add extra sweet chile sauce and some shredded baby spinach leaves to taste.

10 Meanwhile, gently heat the pancakes in a low oven. Serve with the tomato sauce in dipping bowls.

 This vegan dish can be served as a main course. Alternatively, the pancakes can be cut into small, bite-sized segments for a buffet.

ingredients 50g/2oz cooked spinach ❘ 300ml/½ pint milk ❘ 1 egg ❘ 125g/4oz flour ❘ salt and freshly ground black pepper ❘ butter for frying ❘ tomato sauce (see page 132) ❘ sweet chile sauce and finely shredded baby spinach leaves, to serve ❘ FOR THE FILLING 3 bunches spring onions ❘ 300g/10oz shiitake mushrooms ❘ 250g/8oz cooked spinach ❘ a little sunflower oil for frying ❘ 2 tablespoons sweet chile sauce ❘ 2 tablespoons sweet soy sauce

fried eggplant & tomato tofu

1 Preheat oven to 150°C (300°F) Gas Mark 2. Cut the eggplants into large dice without peeling them. Heat some oil in a deep-fat fryer and deep fry until crispy, about 3 minutes. Place the eggplants on a cooling rack in a roasting pan and slowly bake in the oven to draw out the oil, about 5 minutes. Alternatively place under the broiler, about 4 minutes.

2 Peel and finely dice the onion, deseed and finely chop the chiles (see page 46) and cut the tomatoes into small dice, about one inch square including the skins.

3 Pick the leaves from the spinach, wash, and leave to drain.

4 Finely shred the cilantro stalks.

5 If using fresh tofu, drain the water away. Dice the tofu into one-inch cubes.

6 Peel and finely chop the garlic. Heat some oil in a large heavy-based saucepan. Gently fry the onion and garlic without coloring, about 2 minutes. Add the tomatoes and cover with a lid. Simmer slowly until all the liquid has dissolved, stirring occasionally. Be careful not to let the sauce burn or catch on the base of the pan.

7 Add the eggplants, tofu, and cilantro. Again, simmer slowly until all the liquid has dissolved, about 10–15 minutes.

8 To serve, finely shred the spinach and add it to the eggplant-tofu mixture. Season to taste and drizzle with soy sauce.

This is a substantial vegetarian dish that can be used as a main course with an accompaniment of Wok-Seared Greens (see page 86). It can also be served as a starter or as a side dish with main courses such as Five-Spiced Cod with Tamarind & Herbs, Caramelized Ginger Chicken, and Crispy Quail with Watercress (see pages 119, 134, and 147).

If available, fried tofu will also work with this dish. Remember to take your time when cooking this dish as the eggplants will act like a sponge and extracting the oil takes a little time.

ingredients 2 large eggplants | a little sunflower oil for frying | 1 large onion | 2 chiles | 500g/1lb plum tomatoes | 500g/1lb spinach | 2 cilantro sprigs, freshly picked (if possible) | 500g/1lb tofu | 2 garlic cloves | 2 tablespoons light soy sauce | salt and freshly ground black pepper

coconut curried vegetables

1 Finely chop and soak the lemongrass in a large bowl of warm water for about 2 hours. This process makes it easier to eat as part of the curried vegetable mixture.

2 Wash, peel, and dice all the vegetables into half-inch cubes. Sweat the curry paste, garlic, onion, lemongrass, seasoning, sugar, and bay leaf in a little oil without coloring, about 3 minutes.

3 Add the turmeric and cook slowly for a few minutes. Then add the celery, butternut squash, sweet potato, and carrot. Cook for 5 minutes more.

4 Stir in the coconut milk and water. Bring to a boil and simmer for 15 minutes, stirring occasionally.

5 Deep fry the diced baking potato until golden, about 3 minutes. Thoroughly drain on kitchen paper.

6 When the vegetable curry is cooked, remove the saucepan from the heat and leave to cool. When cool, add the deep-fried potato and allow to cool.

7 Thoroughly reheat before serving, then finely shred the spring onions and sprinkle on top.

To allow the full flavor to infuse, this curry should be made about three hours in advance. Curry paste is a vital ingredient in this curried vegetable dish and is available from Asian food stores and some supermarkets. Most cans of coconut milk are available in 400ml/14fl oz cans. The quantities listed here will give you four side dishes, two starter dishes, or one main course.

ingredients 1 stick of lemongrass ▌ 1 sweet potato ▌ 1 carrot ▌ 1 stick of celery ▌ 1 butternut squash (or substitute pumpkin) ▌ 1 baking potato ▌ 1 onion ▌ a little sunflower oil for frying ▌ 1 tablespoon green curry paste ▌ 1 garlic clove, peeled and finely chopped ▌ 1 teaspoon each: salt and freshly ground black pepper ▌ 1 tablespoon superfine sugar ▌ 1 bay leaf, freshly picked (if possible) ▌ 2 tablespoons turmeric powder ▌ 400ml/14fl oz canned coconut milk ▌ 100ml/3½fl oz water ▌ TO GARNISH 2 spring onions

spicy herbed leaf salad

1 Pick the leaves from the mizuna and watercress. Wash, drain, and combine them in a large bowl.

2 Pick the leaves from the mint and cilantro, then wash and drain them. Combine with the watercress and mizuna. Repeat with the basil.

3 Top and tail the chile. Roll it between your hands and shake it. This will remove the seeds. Slice into fine rings.

4 To serve, combine the chile rings with the salad leaves and fold in the Nuoc Cham. Serve immediately.

Leave the tips of the stalks on the herbs to add texture to the salad. Try to select young, tender herbs as the larger herbs have tougher leaves. Chile adds color and a spicy taste to this dish. Unlike ordinary basil, Asian basil lends an anise seed flavor.

This salad can be served as a vegetarian starter or as an accompaniment to Mushroom & Rice-stuffed Cabbage, Five-Spiced Cod with Tamarind & Herbs, and Curried Frog's Legs (see pages 94, 119, and 123).

ingredients 2 bunches each: mizuna (or young and tender arugula leaves) and watercress | 1 bunch each: mint, cilantro, and Asian basil, freshly picked (if possible) | 1 large red chile | 120ml/4fl oz vegetarian Nuoc Cham (see page 57)

mushroom & rice-stuffed cabbage

1 Make the tomato sauce, but omit the sweet chile sauce. Pick, wash, and finely shred the watercress and add to the sauce.

2 Remove the outer leaves from the cabbage, keeping them whole. Rinse and pat dry with paper towels. For this recipe you will need 8 leaves.

3 Bring a large heavy-based saucepan of salted water to a boil and blanch the leaves for about 10 seconds. Refresh in cold water.

4 Wipe and finely slice the mushrooms. Shred the spring onions, and deseed and finely dice the chiles. Drain the water chestnuts and chop into small pieces.

5 Heat a wok and when hot, add the vegetable oil. Fry the ingredients in step 4 for about 2 minutes. Season well.

6 Allow the mixture to cool slightly, then mix with the rice. Add 2 tablespoons tomato sauce and check the seasoning. Allow to cool.

7 Open out each of the cabbage leaves and divide the filling between them. Wrap, tucking the leaf edge underneath. Trim as necessary. Leave to rest for about 1 hour in the refrigerator before serving.

8 To reheat the stuffed cabbage leaves, either steam or preheat oven to 150°C (300°F) Gas Mark 2 and place the leaves on a baking sheet. Bake (or steam) for 7–10 minutes. Meanwhile, reheat the remaining sauce.

9 To serve, divide the sauce between 4 plates and place 2 stuffed cabbage leaves on top. Garnish with fresh cilantro leaves.

This is a perfect vegetarian dish or an alternative main course. Since the leaves are full of rice, serve with Wok-Seared Greens (see page 86) for a nice balance.

ingredients tomato sauce (see page 132) ▌ 1 large bunch watercress ▌ 1 medium Napa cabbage ▌ 500g/1lb shiitake mushrooms ▌ 4 spring onions ▌ 2 red chiles ▌ 250g/8oz canned water chestnuts ▌ a little vegetable oil for frying ▌ 300g/10oz Sticky Rice, cooked (see page 60) ▌ salt and freshly ground black pepper ▌ FOR THE GARNISH cilantro leaves, freshly picked (if possible)

fish & seafood

"In the sector reserved for food is every variety of fresh, dried, and smoked fish: huge, with silver undersides, medium size threaded on a stick, and crabs from the rice fields like copper coins swarming in great enamel basins."

Vietnamiennes au Quotidien, Francoise Corrèze, 1982

crab & asparagus soup

1 In a small bowl, pick through the crab meat and remove any remaining shell pieces.

2 Rinse and chop the asparagus into small pieces, stalk and slice the shiitake mushrooms, then shred and wash the bok choy.

3 Finely shred the cilantro and slice the chile in half lengthwise. Deseed and finely slice the chile.

4 In a large heavy-based saucepan, bring the chicken stock to a boil. Add the crab meat, asparagus, bok choy, mushrooms, fish sauce, cilantro, and black pepper. Return the soup to a boil, stirring. The soup is now cooked.

5 To serve, ladle the soup into serving bowls and sprinkle with chile slices. Divide the lime into quarters and serve with the soup.

 Ensure the crab meat is the freshest available as this will add extra flavor to the soup. The chile and pepper can be increased or decreased to your desired taste. White asparagus makes this dish more attractive. If unavailable, use green. The bok choy and cilantro are shredded to make them easier to eat as a soup.

ingredients 125g/4oz white crab meat | 125g/4oz white asparagus tips | 200g/8oz shiitake mushrooms | 2 heads of bok choy | 12 sprigs of cilantro, freshly picked (if possible) | 1 small red chile | 750ml/1¼ pints Chicken Stock (see page 64) | 4 tablespoons fish sauce | 1 teaspoon ground black pepper | FOR THE GARNISH 1 lime

crispy marinated squid with bitter lemon dressing

1   Peel the garlic cloves and rinse the dill. Roughly chop the two together in a blender or food processor. Transfer to a large bowl and stir in the fish sauce.

2   Stir in the squid and peppercorns. Cover and leave to marinate for at least 6 hours in the refrigerator.

3   In a large bowl, mix together the flour and cornstarch. Remove the squid from the marinade with a slotted spoon and coat it thoroughly in the flour mixture.

4   Heat some oil in a deep fat fryer and fry the squid until crispy, about 3 minutes. Drain on paper towels.

5   To serve, arrange the squid on individual plates. Garnish with lime quarters or halves and serve with small dipping bowls of Bitter Lemon Dressing.

This squid dish makes an ideal starter. It could also be served as a small main course along with Stir-Fried Ginger Noodles and Wok-Seared Greens (see pages 83 and 86).

ingredients   3 garlic cloves | 1 bunch dill, freshly picked (if possible) | 6 tablespoons fish sauce | 300g/10oz squid bodies and tentacles | 1 tablespoon ground black peppercorns | 4 tablespoons flour | 4 tablespoons cornstarch | a little vegetable or sunflower oil for deep frying | 8 tablespoons Bitter Lemon Dressing (see page 55) | FOR THE GARNISH 4 limes, cut into quarters or halved

sesame prawns with sour green mango salad

1 Peel the prawns, leaving the tails on for the garnish. Cut through the meat in the center near the top and slice down to the tails to leave them attached to the tops and bottoms. Devein the prawns, then turn the tails through the prawns inside out to leave a twisted appearance. Refrigerate, covered, until needed.

2 Peel and shred the mango into long, thin strips. Then peel and cut the cucumber into strips. Combine the two in a large bowl.

3 In a separate bowl, combine the sesame seeds and Panko breadcrumbs. Combine the flour, egg whites, and soy sauce in another bowl.

4 Pass the prawns through the flour mixture. Then pass them through the breadcrumb mixture to coat completely.

5 Pick and wash the mizuna leaves and leave to drain.

6 Cut the chile in half lengthwise, deseed, and finely slice.

7 Heat the oil an, when hot, deep fry the prawns, about 1 minute; drain on paper towels.

8 To serve, arrange the mizuna leaves around a serving dish. In a bowl, combine the mango and cucumber with the Nuoc Cham and chile, then arrange in a pile on top of the leaves. Place the prawns around the garnish, tails facing outwards to make them easier to pick up and to add to the presentation. Serve with extra Nuoc Cham in dipping bowls, if desired.

Serve as a starter dish. 1kg/2lb should allow for about 16 prawns, enough for a starter portion. Panko breadcrumbs are dried white breadcrumbs that originate from Asia. They add extra crispiness to this dish.

ingredients 16 raw prawns | 1 sour green mango, available from Asian stores | 1 cucumber | 1 bunch of mizuna (or young and tender arugula leaves), freshly picked (if possible) | 1 large red chile | a little sunflower or vegetable oil for deep frying | 3 tablespoons Nuoc Cham (see page 57), plus extra for serving, if desired | FOR THE SESAME COATING 3 tablespoons white sesame seeds | 2 tablespoons black sesame seeds | 3 tablespoons Japanese Panko breadcrumbs | 4 tablespoons flour | 2 egg whites | 2 tablespoons light soy sauce

soft-shell crabs with mizuna & pomelo

1 To make the Spiced Flour, in a large heavy-based frying pan toast the coriander and cumin seeds until cooked, about 3 minutes. Grind the two seeds together. Transfer to a large bowl and combine with the remaining ingredients for the flour.

2 Peel and segment the pomelos, then cut the segments into halves.

3 Wash the mizuna leaves and leave to drain thoroughly.

4 In a large bowl, combine the pomelo pieces, mizuna leaves, and Nuoc Cham.

5 Toss the crabs in the flour to coat them. Heat the oil and deep fry the crabs until crispy, about 1 minute for medium-sized crabs.

6 To serve, arrange a bamboo leaf on each plate and divide the chive stems between plates. Place equal amounts of pomelo garnish on each plate and top with the crispy crab.

This dish is ideal served as a light appetizer. It would also make a perfect main course meal on a warm summer's evening.

ingredients 2 large pomelos or sour grapefruits | 1 bunch mizuna (or young and tender arugula leaves), freshly picked (if possible) | 3 tablespoons Nuoc Cham (see page 57) | 4 medium soft-shell or boneless crab claws | 4 tablespoons Spiced Flour (see below) | a little sunflower or vegetable oil for deep frying | 4 bamboo leaves, available from Asian stores | 8 stems of Chinese chives | FOR THE SPICED FLOUR 2 tablespoons each: coriander seeds and cumin seeds, paprika, potato flour, and flour | 1 tablespoon each: chile powder and freshly ground black pepper | 1 tablespoon coarse sea salt | 2 tablespoons Japanese Panko breadcrumbs

raw marinated salmon with cucumber & cilantro

1 Cover the prepared salmon flesh in plastic wrap. Refrigerate for a maximum of 1 hour.

2 Peel the mouli and slice it lengthwise as finely as possible.

3 Peel the cucumber and slice it in half lengthwise. Deseed and slice in the same way as the mouli.

4 Wash and pick the cilantro into small sprigs.

5 In a large heavy-based frying pan, dry roast the whitest rice you can buy over a low heat to cook slowly. When nice and brown, about 10 minutes, pass through a grinder. This process will take a little while so be patient.

6 Slice the salmon as finely as possible (as for smoked salmon).

7 To serve, arrange the salmon around each plate. Sprinkle cucumber and mouli on top in no particular fashion. Drizzle Nuoc Cham lightly over the salmon. Loosely arrange cilantro sprigs on the top and finish with a sprinkling of rice powder.

The rice powder makes a lovely addition to this dish and is well worth making. For best results, slice the salmon as finely as possible.

This recipe is ideal as a light starter or as part of a selection of different dishes for a buffet party, such as Grilled Chicken Brochettes with Lemongrass Noodles, Crispy Marinated Squid with Bitter Lemon Dressing, and Sesame Prawns with Sour Green Mango Salad (see pages 76, 101, and 102).

ingredients 2 x 175g/6oz salmon fillets, skinned with the underside cut away to reveal the dark flesh (your fishmonger can do this for you) ❙ 1 mouli (Chinese radish) ❙ 1 cucumber ❙ 1 bunch cilantro, freshly picked (if possible) ❙ 4 teaspoons roasted rice powder (see method) ❙ 120ml/4fl oz Nuoc Cham (see page 57)

broiled fillet of sole wrapped in banana leaves

1   Preheat oven to 180°C (350°F) Gas Mark 4.
    Meanwhile, blanch the banana leaves in boiling
    water, about 1 minute.

2   Season the sole fillets and fold each one up
    lengthwise into three.

3   Place each fillet, serving side up, diagonally inside a
    banana leaf, season, and sprinkle with Nuoc Cham.

4   Fold the four corners of each leaf into the center
    and place seamside down in a roasting pan or an
    ovenproof dish. Bake in a hot oven for about 10–15
    minutes, or until just slightly undercooked.

5   Use a spatula to turn each sole parcel over gently
    (be careful not to break the fish). Open the parcels
    and place under a hot broiler or return to the oven
    for 5 minutes.

6   To serve, place a sole fillet, still in its banana-leaf
    parcel, in the center of each plate. Drizzle with
    Lemongrass Dressing to garnish.

ingredients 4 x 20cm/8in banana leaf squares, available from Asian stores ❙ 4 x 500g/1lb sole fillets, skins removed and pinboned (your fishmonger can do this for you) ❙ salt and freshly ground black pepper ❙ 2½ tablespoons Nuoc Cham (see page 57) ❙ 120ml/4fl oz Lemongrass Dressing (see page 52)

cha-ca monkfish with turmeric, dill & onion

1   Slice the monkfish tails into large rounds. To do this, start from the pointed tip ends and work at a slight angle. This will give you nice long discs and an even cut of fish as well.

2   Peel the garlic and the galangal. In a food processor, blend together the galangal and garlic. Stir in the yogurt and turmeric.

3   Stir in the monkfish discs, cover, and leave to marinate for at least 5 hours in the refrigerator.

4   Peel and finely slice the onions (the finer the better) and pick the dill into large pieces.

5   Heat some oil in a large heavy-based frying pan. Add the monkfish and fry quickly until brown, about 4 minutes. Stir in the onion slices.

6   Just before serving, stir in the dill and Nuoc Cham.

7   To serve, arrange the monkfish mixture in the center of each plate. Garnish with halved limes and a little of the remaining sauce from the frying pan.

Try to avoid getting turmeric on your hands as it stains and is not easy to remove. This dish would be great served with a side portion of Sticky Rice or Stir-Fried Ginger Noodles (see pages 60 and 83).

ingredients   4 x 250g/8oz monkfish tails, cleaned (your fishmonger can do this for you) **❙** 4 garlic cloves **❙** 1 large galangal stem **❙** 50ml/2fl oz Greek yogurt **❙** 12 tablespoons turmeric **❙** 2 large onions **❙** 1 large bunch of dill, freshly picked (if possible) **❙** vegetable or sunflower oil for frying **❙** 3 tablespoons Nuoc Cham (see page 57) **❙** FOR THE GARNISH 2 limes

grilled salmon with coconut curry & Hanoi vegetables

1   To make the curry sauce, grind the cumin and coriander seeds to a powder and finely shred the lime and bay leaves and lemongrass.

2   Peel and finely dice the garlic clove and shallot.

3   Melt some butter in a large heavy-based frying pan and fry the above prepared ingredients without coloring, about 3 minutes. Stir in the curry paste and turmeric and cook, stirring, about 3 minutes.

4   Pour in the chicken stock and bring to a boil. Reduce the heat slightly. Stir in the coconut milk and reduce the mixture to form the consistency of a sauce. Pass through a fine sieve into a saucepan, using a spoon or small ladle to push out as much of the flavor as possible.

5   For the Hanoi vegetables, peel and cut the papaya and cucumber in half lengthwise; deseed. Cut into fine dice. Peel the shallot, cut it in half lengthwise and finely slice.

6   Thoroughly wash and rewash the mustard greens.

7   Lightly season the salmon. Cook on a grill if available to reproduce the attractive markings on the fish or pan-fry in a little sunflower oil to retain the moisture in the fish.

8   For best results, cook the vegetables in a wok. Heat some oil until it becomes hot, then add all the vegetables at once. Quickly stir-fry for about 30 seconds and drain.

9   To serve, arrange the vegetables around the base of a serving dish. Top with salmon and pour the sauce around the fish or serve it separately.

 This dish could be served with accompaniments of Sticky Rice, Stir-fried Ginger Noodles, and Wok-Seared Greens (see pages 60, 83, and 86).

ingredients 4 x 185g/6½oz salmon fillets, scaled and pinboned (your fishmonger can do this for you) | a little sunflower oil for frying | salt and freshly ground black pepper | FOR THE CURRY SAUCE 1 tablespoon each: whole cumin and coriander seeds | 2 kaffir lime leaves | 3 bay leaves, freshly picked (if possible) | 2 sticks of lemongrass | 1 garlic clove | 1 large shallot | a little butter for frying | 1 tablespoon green curry paste | 2 tablespoons ground turmeric | 750ml/1¼ pints Chicken Stock (see page 64) | 2 x 400ml/14fl oz cans coconut milk | FOR THE HANOI VEGETABLES 1 green papaya | 1 cucumber | 1 large shallot | 250g/8oz mustard greens, freshly picked (if possible)

spiced crab & spinach cakes with galangal sauce

1 Preheat oven to 180°C (350°F) Gas Mark 4. Rinse the potato skin, prick it with a fork and wrap it in foil. Bake for about 1 hour until cooked.

2 Meanwhile, in a bowl, pick over the crab meat with a fork to ensure that there are no remaining bones.

3 Top and tail, peel, and finely shred the spring onions. Slice the chile in half lengthwise, deseed, and dice. Strip the leaves from the cilantro and finely chop. Add to the bowl.

4 When the potato is cooked, remove the foil. Cut a cross in the top, allow to cool slightly, then scoop out the mashed potato into a large bowl. Mash instantly with a fork or potato masher in order to keep a smooth texture (if you allow the potato to cool too much, the mash will start to become sticky and elastic).

5 Pick over and wash the spinach leaves; divide into two. Heat some oil in a hot wok or large heavy-based frying pan. Toss half the spinach in the oil until cooked, about 1 minute. Drain and squeeze out as much liquid as possible. Finely chop and add to the rest of the ingredients in the bowl; season and combine thoroughly.

6 Leave the mixture to cool and then weigh out the fish cakes individually (allow 80g/3¼oz each to yield 8 cakes).

7 In another bowl, whisk together the eggs and milk. Spoon the flour out onto a large plate and place the breadcrumbs on another plate.

8 Shape the fishcakes using a palette knife or the side of an ordinary knife. Pass each cake through the flour, shaking off the excess, then dip into the egg mixture and coat with breadcrumbs. Reshape as before and set aside while you prepare the sauce.

9 Make the Galangal Sauce.

10 Fry the crab cakes in hot oil in either a deep fat fryer or large heavy-based frying pan for about

ingredients 1 large potato **|** 275g/9oz fresh white crab meat **|** 4 spring onions **|** 1 red chile **|** 1 bunch of cilantro, freshly picked (if possible) **|** 350g/11½oz spinach **|** a little vegetable oil for frying **|** 2 eggs **|** 2 tablespoons milk **|** 8 tablespoons flour **|** 4 tablespoons Japanese Panko breadcrumbs **|** 1 teaspoon each: salt and freshly ground black pepper **|** Galangal Sauce (see page 58)

4 minutes, turning until crispy and golden. Heat some more oil in a wok or large heavy-based frying pan. Season and quickly toss the spinach in the oil, about 7 minutes, then drain.

11 To serve, place a pile of cooked spinach on each plate, place two crab cakes on top and spoon or drizzle a little of the sauce around the plate. (Do not allow any sauce to get on the cakes if deep fried or else they will become soggy.)

To give this dish a little extra zip, pass four crispy crab claws through the flour, egg, and breadcrumb mixtures and deep fry or pan-fry, about 1 minute, to garnish.

One very large potato should give you almost equal quantities of crab meat to potato. Alternatively, boil the potato and drain and dry in a low oven (about 170°C (325°F) Gas Mark 3) before mashing. Panko breadcrumbs not only give a different texture; they also soak up any moisture left in the mixture to give firm cakes. If unavailable, dry out some fresh bread and crumble it in a blender as an alternative.

Serve with Stir-Fried Ginger Noodles (see page 83).

peppered tuna with sour tomato & lemon

1   In a large shallow bowl, roll the tuna loin through the pepper.

2   Heat a large heavy-based frying pan and, when hot, add the oil. Sear the tuna in the pan for a few seconds on each side, leaving the center raw. Allow to cool, then cover and refrigerate.

3   Place the tomatoes in a bowl of boiling salted water for 10 seconds to blanch them. Remove with a slotted spoon; peel, deseed, and cut into small dice.

4   Peel and finely chop the garlic and shallots.

5   Peel and juice the lemons. Dice the peelings as finely as possible.

6   Heat a large heavy-based saucepan, add some oil and sweat the shallot, garlic, and tomatoes. Allow to stew for about 5 minutes over low heat. Add the sake, Nuoc Cham, lemon rind, and juice. Leave to stew until all the liquid has dissolved, stirring occasionally.

7   Season the mixture to taste. Remove from the heat and set aside to cool.

8   Pick over the mizuna. Wash and allow to drain.

9   With a sharp knife, finely slice the tuna to create small, thin slices rather than long ones. To do this, cut down through the thin width of the meat and allow about 4 slices per portion.

10   To serve, arrange the mizuna on a serving dish and spoon some of the tomato mixture over the top. Place the tuna in fan-shaped layers so that it falls away from the tomato. Quarter and deseed the remaining lemon. Garnish with lemon quarters and cilantro sprigs.

Use the freshest tuna available. Most fishmongers are able to provide really fresh tuna. To add to the flavor, grind your own black pepper. This dish can be sweetened by adding a teaspoon of sugar to the tomato mixture as it cools down.

ingredients 375g/12oz tuna loin ▮ 4 tablespoons freshly ground black pepper ▮ a little sunflower or vegetable oil for frying ▮ 500g/1lb plum tomatoes ▮ 2 garlic cloves ▮ 2 large shallots ▮ 2 lemons ▮ 2 tablespoons sake ▮ 8 tablespoons Nuoc Cham (see page 57) ▮ 1 bunch mizuna (or young and tender arugula leaves), freshly picked (if possible) ▮ salt and freshly ground black pepper ▮ FOR THE GARNISH 1 lemon ▮ 4 cilantro sprigs, freshly picked (if possible)

five-spiced cod with tamarind & herbs

1   Pick over the watercress, cilantro, mizuna leaves, basil, and mint. Wash and combine together in a large bowl.

2   In a large shallow bowl, combine the flour and five spice powder. Roll the cod steaks through it to coat them with flour.

3   Preheat oven to 150–170°C (300–325°F) Gas Mark 2–3. Meanwhile, heat some oil in a large heavy-based frying pan and when hot, seal the cod, about 1 minute on each side. Bake the cod, uncovered, in the oven, about 5 minutes.

4   To serve, place a portion of herbs and leaves on each plate (or serve in the bowl). Cut the limes in half. Place a cod steak on each plate and serve the Tamarind Sauce in individual dipping bowls beside each steak with two lime halves.

The skin needs to be left on because as the cod cooks it will become crispy. This adds to the texture of the dish and also helps to keep the fish moist. It can easily be removed after cooking.

The herbs and leaves can also be served as an accompaniment to other dishes such as Vietnamese Hot Pot, Cha-Ca Monkfish with Turmeric, Dill & Onion, or Barbecued Pork Ribs with Hoisin Sauce (see pages 79, 110, and 144), to name but a few. Other side dishes that will go with this recipe include Sticky Rice and Stir-Fried Ginger Noodles (see pages 60 and 83).

ingredients 2 bunches of watercress ▎ 1 bunch each: cilantro, mizuna (or young and tender arugula leaves), Asian basil, and mint, freshly picked (if possible) ▎ 4 tablespoons flour ▎ 8 tablespoons five spice powder ▎ 4 x 185g/6½oz cod steaks, skin on but scaled and pinboned (your fishmonger can do this for you) ▎ a little sunflower oil for frying ▎ FOR THE GARNISH 4 limes ▎ 175ml/6fl oz Tamarind Sauce (see page 65)

shrimp on sugar cane

1 To make the prawn paste, chop the prawn tails. Discard the rind from the pork fat and finely chop.

2 Peel and roughly chop the shallot and garlic.

3 Place the above ingredients in the bowl of a food processor. Process until smooth, about 2 minutes.

4 Add the egg white, fish sauce, seasoning, cornstarch, and rice powder. Blend again to incorporate the ingredients. Place the mixture, covered, in the refrigerator for about 10 minutes.

5 If using canned sugar cane, cut each stick into quarters and trim the edges, allowing 3 sticks, or "skewers," per person.

6 Divide the mixture (allow 50g/2oz per skewer). Roll each one into a ball. Press the ball with the cup of your hand to create a small disc and wrap it around a cane stick. Repeat until all the canes are wrapped, then place in the refrigerator, uncovered, for another 10 minutes until hardened.

7 Smooth each cane by placing a little oil in the cup of your hand. Roll the canes through it, leaving a space at each end (to make them easier to hold).

8 Peel and finely slice the onion. Wash the lettuce leaves and shred the mint. Combine the onion and mint in a bowl.

9 If possible, cook the skewers on a grill, about 3 minutes on each side. This will give a great taste and appearance. Alternatively, deep fry or pan fry, about 1 minute or place under a broiler, about 2 minutes.

10 To serve, place a lettuce leaf on each plate, top with three skewers and sprinkle with the onion–mint mixture. Serve with small dipping bowls of Nuoc Cham on the side. To eat this dish, remove the mousse from the sugar cane and garnish. Chew the cane to extract the sugar.

Pork fat may be substituted for chicken. The fat not only adds flavor; it also helps to keep the skewers bound together. Fresh sugar cane is difficult to work with. When cutting it, be sure to use a very sharp serrated knife

ingredients 500g/1lb meat from prawn tails, deveined (your fishmonger can do this for you) ▎ 50g/2oz pork fat ▎ 1 large shallot ▎ 2 garlic cloves ▎ 1 egg white ▎ 2 tablespoons fish sauce ▎ 1 teaspoon each: salt and freshly ground black pepper ▎ 2 tablespoons cornstarch ▎ 2 tablespoons roasted rice powder (see Raw Marinated Salmon, page 106) ▎ 1 x 500g/1lb can (if available) sugar cane (if freshly available, use 2 sticks) ▎ a little sunflower oil ▎ 1 small white onion ▎ 4 iceberg lettuce leaves ▎ 1 bunch of mint, freshly picked (if possible) ▎ 120ml/4fl oz Nuoc Cham (see page 57)

curried frogs' legs

1   To make the sauce, peel and finely chop the shallot, ginger, and garlic.

2   In a large heavy-based frying pan, dry roast the coriander and cumin seeds; grind to a powder.

3   In a large heavy-based saucepan, sweat the shallot, ginger, and garlic without color, about 1 minute in 1 tablespooon oil. Add the ground seeds, bay leaves, and tomato purée. Cook, stirring, for 2 minutes.

4   Add the vegetable stock, coconut milk, and Tamarind Sauce. Stir and bring the mixture to the boil. Leave to simmer for 10 minutes.

5   Season the mixture and remove from the heat. Stir in the yogurt and pass the sauce through a large fine sieve into a bowl. Make sure you push all the flavor out of the vegetables.

6   Meanwhile, in a large bowl, combine the flour and cornstarch. Pass the frogs' legs through this. Deep fry for about 3 minutes until golden and crispy.

7   To serve, pour a pool of sauce onto each plate, arrange the frogs' legs in a pile on top and garnish with a sprig of mint. Serve the extra curry sauce in small pots.

Frogs' legs are now available frozen and are readily available from supermarkets and some fishmongers. Sticky Rice, Stir-fried Ginger Noodles, or Wok-Seared Greens (see pages 60, 83 and 86) work well with this dish. Quantities can be halved to make starter portions.

ingredients   125g/4oz flour | 125g/4oz corstarch | 1.25kg/2½lb frogs' legs (allow 6 legs per portion) | a little vegetable or sunflower oil for frying | 4 mint sprigs, freshly picked (if possible), to garnish | FOR THE CURRY SAUCE 1 large shallot | 1 stem of ginger | 1 garlic clove | 1 teaspoon each: coriander and cumin seeds | a little sunflower oil | 2 bay leaves, freshly picked (if possible) | 2 tablespoons tomato purée | 250ml/8floz vegetable stock | 400ml/14fl oz coconut milk | 4 tablespoons Tamarind Sauce (see page 65) | 1 teaspoon each: salt and freshly ground black pepper | 5 tablespoons plain yogurt

muc nhoi stuffed squid

1 Cut the squid tentacles into small pieces and mix them in a large bowl with the prawn paste and spring roll mix.

2 Stuff the squid tubes with this mixture and seal with two cocktail sticks criss crossed across the end. Place them on a plate and refrigerate for 15 minutes to set.

3 Meanwhile, in a large heavy-based saucepan of boiling salted water cook the vermicelli for 2 minutes or until al dente. Drain and cool under cold running water.

4 Peel and grate the carrot lengthwise. Cut the cucumber in half lengthwise, deseed, and finely shred. Then cut the chile in half, deseed, and finely dice. In a bowl, combine all these ingredients and stir in the noodles.

5 Preheat oven to 160–180°C (325–350°F) Gas Mark 3–4. Meanwhile, deep fry the squid in hot oil until crispy, about 1 minute. Place on a baking sheet and finish off in the oven for 10 minutes to ensure the filling is thoroughly cooked. Leave to rest for 5 minutes.

6 To serve, add 4 tablespoons Nuoc Cham to the noodle mixture, stir, and then place in four piles on serving dishes. Slice the squid into bite-sized pieces and arrange around the noodles. (Discard the top and tail: this should give you four slices.) Garnish with lime halves and cilantro sprigs. Peel, slice in half lengthwise, and finely shred the shallot; add to the noodles. Serve with small pots of Nuoc Cham dipping sauce.

 Use the freshest squid available. Older squid has a sandy texture. If tentacles are not available, chop up and use a few prawn tails instead.

This is an ideal starter or summer salad dish. Serve with Grilled Chicken Brochettes with Lemongrass Noodles or Crispy Smoked Chicken with Fragrant Greens (see pages 76 and 128).

ingredients 4 x 125g/4oz squid tentacles and tubes ▎ 4 tablespoons prawn paste (see Shrimp on Sugar Cane, page 120) ▎ 125g/4oz spring roll mix (see Crispy Spring Roll, page 74) ▎ 50g/2oz rice vermicelli noodles ▎ 1 carrot ▎ 1 cucumber ▎ 1 red chile ▎ a little sunflower oil ▎ 175ml/6fl oz Nuoc Cham (see page 57) ▎ 2 limes, halved ▎ 4 cilantro sprigs, freshly picked (if possible) and 1 large shallot, to garnish

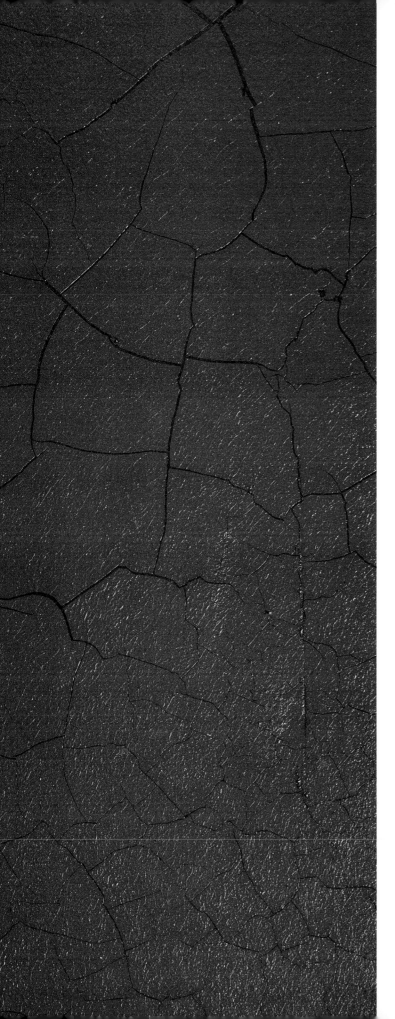

meat & poultry

"After the cha gio came a flux of delicacies,

designed undoubtedly to provoke curiosity

and admiration and to provide the excuse

for enormously prolonged dalliance at the

table rather than to appease gross

appetites."

The Dragon Apparent, Norman Lewis, *1951*

crispy smoked chicken with fragrant greens

1 Use your fingers to pick the chicken into small strips.

2 Finely shred the spring greens. Heat some sunflower oil in a deep-fat fryer and deep fry the greens for a few seconds until crispy, about 1 minute, and drain on kitchen paper.

3 Slice the chiles in half lengthwise, deseed, and finely slice. Peel the shallots and slice into thin rings.

4 Thoroughly wash the cilantro and shred the stems.

5 Heat some oil in a large heavy-based saucepan and sauté the shallots and chiles until soft, about 2 minutes. Remove the saucepan from the heat and when the mixture has cooled, stir in the cilantro. Set aside.

6 In a large bowl, combine the soy sauce with the water. Mix the flour and cornstarch together in a separate bowl.

7 Remove the leaves from the bok choy, wash the stems, and shred finely. (The leaves can be used in other dishes.)

8 Pass the chicken strips through the soy sauce mixture and coat with flour. Heat some sunflower oil in a large heavy-based frying pan and fry the chicken strips until crisp, about 3 minutes. Drain on paper towels.

9 In a large bowl, combine the crispy greens, shredded bok choy, and the shallot-cilantro mixture. Add half the dressing and mix together thoroughly.

10 To serve, arrange the prepared mixture around the center of each plate, top with crispy chicken, and garnish with a lemon wedge. Serve the remaining dressing in separate dipping bowls.

 Serve with Spicy Noodle Salad (see page 80).

ingredients 400g/13oz smoked chicken meat ▌ 2 spring greens ▌ a little sunflower oil for frying ▌ 2 red chiles ▌ 2 large shallots ▌ 1 small bunch of cilantro, freshly picked (if possible) ▌ 8 tablespoons light soy sauce ▌ 4 tablespoons water ▌ 4 tablespoons each: flour and cornstarch ▌ 3 heads of bok choy ▌ 600ml/1 pint Lime & Rice Wine Vinegar Dressing (see page 54) ▌ 1 lemon, cut into 4 wedges

spicy raw beef with aromatic basil, lime & chile

1 Arrange the beef slices carefully around the plates. Season with salt and pepper.

2 Sprinkle the shallots, chile, and basil randomly over the beef.

3 Drizzle with lime juice and Nuoc Cham.

4 To serve, sprinkle ground rice powder lightly over each plate to give the dish a texture that everyone will love.

 Pickled bean sprouts are a perfect accompaniment to this dish.

ingredients 300g/10oz beef striploin, sliced carpaccio-thin (your butcher can do this for you) ❘ 60g/2½oz shallots, finely sliced ❘ 1 red chile, finely sliced and deseeded ❘ 4 Asian sweet basil sprigs, freshly picked (if possible) and torn into small pieces ❘ 4 tablespoons lime juice ❘ 4 tablespoons Nuoc Cham (see page 57) ❘ salt and freshly ground black pepper ❘FOR THE GARNISH roasted rice powder (see page 106)

farchiew pork fillet

1 Grind the Farchiew spice and dried red chile together (using mortar and pestle) and combine with the seasoning. Transfer to a shallow bowl and use to coat the pork fillets.

2 Place the tomatoes in a bowl of boiling salted water for 10 seconds to blanch them. Remove with a slotted spoon; peel, deseed, and dice. Peel and finely chop the shallots and garlic.

3 Heat some sunflower oil in a large heavy-based frying pan and sauté the shallot and garlic until golden, about 2 minutes. Add the diced tomatoes and leave to simmer for about 10 minutes.

4 Meanwhile, finely shred the basil and deseed and finely chop the green chile. Add them to the pan.

5 Remove from the heat and stir in the sweet chile sauce.

6 Add some sunflower oil to a hot, heavy-based frying pan and fry the pork fillets until colored on both sides and cooked completely, about 3 minutes. Remove from the pan, allow to rest for 5 minutes on paper towels, then finely slice.

7 To serve, spoon a pool of tomato sauce onto each serving dish and arrange the pork slices on top. Garnish with watercress.

To cook the pork more quickly and to give a fuller flavor, butterfly the fillets before rolling them through the spice. To do this, cut lengthwise through the fillet all the way through, then unfold (or ask your butcher to do this for you).

Farchiew spice is similar to Szechuan spice and is part of the pepper family.

ingredients 2 tablespoons Farchiew spice ▎ 1 dried red chile ▎ 1 teaspoon each: salt and freshly ground black pepper ▎ 4 x 125g/4oz pork fillet steaks or loin chops ▎ 500g/1lb plum tomatoes ▎ 2 large shallots ▎ 1 garlic clove ▎ a little sunflower oil for frying ▎ 1 sprig Asian sweet basil, freshly picked (if possible) ▎ 1 green chile ▎ 1 tablespoon sweet chile sauce ▎ FOR THE GARNISH 1 bunch watercress

caramelized ginger chicken

1   Cut each chicken thigh into three equal pieces. Place in a large bowl with the ginger, two-thirds of the oil, and seasoning. Cover and marinate for about 6 hours in the refrigerator.

2   Heat a large heavy-based frying pan and pour in the remaining oil. Leave to heat through, then add the chicken. Fry until the meat is colored, about 2 minutes, then drain away the excess oil.

3   Add the fish sauce, cover the pan with a lid, and steam until the sauce has dissolved, about 1 minute.

4   Now add the prepared caramel to the pan and cook until the caramel has thickened and coated the chicken in a rich golden color, about 2 minutes, stirring occasionally.

5   To serve, arrange the chicken pieces on a serving platter and garnish with watercress.

 Stir-Fried Ginger Noodles or Wok-Seared Greens (see pages 83 and 86) would go well as accompaniments to this dish.

ingredients 12 meaty chicken thighs, boned and trimmed with skins still on (your butcher can do this for you) | 200g/7oz fresh ginger, peeled and finely shredded | 100ml/3½fl oz sunflower oil | 6 tablespoons fish sauce | 50ml/2fl oz caramel (see Sesame Banana Fritters, page 162) | salt and freshly ground black pepper | FOR THE GARNISH 4 large watercress sprigs

chicken & cashew stir-fry

1   Cut the chicken supremes into even strips. Peel the shallots and carrots, slice them lengthwise, and cut into slices.

2   Wash and roughly chop the bok choy. Peel and slice the spring onion.

3   Preheat oven to 220°C (425°F) Gas Mark 7. Roast the cashew nuts, uncovered on a baking sheet, for a few minutes until crunchy.

4   Slice the baby corn into large pieces. Chop the dried chiles into small pieces and leave to soak for about 10 minutes in water.

5   Wash the bean sprouts thoroughly and leave to drain in a large sieve.

6   Heat some oil in a large heavy-based frying pan and, when hot, drain the chiles and cook together with the seasoned chicken. Coat with 4 tablespoons soy sauce and set aside.

7   In a large heavy-based wok, heat some more oil and cook all the remaining ingredients apart from the cashew nuts and bean sprouts. Add the chicken and chiles to the wok and stir to incorporate all the ingredients together.

8   Mix in the cashew nuts and bean sprouts. Stir in the remaining soy sauce.

9   To serve, garnish with cilantro sprig tips and serve immediately.

 Serve with either Sticky Rice or Stir-Fried Ginger Noodles (see pages 60 and 83).
The chiles may be omitted or increased to your own desired taste.

ingredients 4 x 250g/8oz chicken breasts, skinned and boned (your butcher can do this for you) **|** 2 large shallots **|** 2 large carrots **|** 4 heads bok choy **|** 1 spring onion **|** 250g/8oz cashew nuts, blanched whole **|** 2 x 50g/2oz packets of baby corn **|** 3 dried chiles **|** 500g/1lb bean sprouts **|** a little sunflower oil for frying **|** 6 tablespoons sweet soy sauce **|** salt and freshly ground black pepper **|** FOR THE GARNISH cilantro sprig tips

sesame lamb & shiitake sauté with mint & shallots

1 Shred the meat into thin strips. The smaller the pieces, the easier the lamb will be to marinate and cook.

2 Peel and chop the garlic and ginger.

3 In a large shallow dish, combine the garlic, ginger, 6 tablespoons of the soy sauce, and the sesame oil. Place the lamb strips in to marinate, covered, for about 6 hours in the refrigerator.

4 Peel the shallots and then cut them lengthwise; finely slice.

5 Chop the pak choy into small pieces; wash it and leave to drain. Wipe and finely slice the mushrooms.

6 In a large heavy-based frying pan, dry roast the sesame seeds (there is sufficient oil inside them already) until golden, about 2 minutes. Grind the seeds and leave to cool.

7 Pick the leaves from the mint and wash and dry them.

8 Heat a dry wok until hot and add the marinated lamb (the oil from the marinade is sufficient for frying). Fry until sealed all over, about 2 minutes. Add the mushrooms, shallots, and pak choy.

9 When the mixture is almost cooked, about 3 minutes, add the remaining soy sauce and stir. Just before serving, stir in the mint leaves.

10 To serve, arrange the sauté on a serving dish and sprinkle with ground sesame seeds.

 Serve with Sticky Rice or Stir-Fried Ginger Noodles and Wok-Seared Greens (see pages 60, 83, and 86).

ingredients 400g/14oz leg of lamb (or rump, fillet, or middle neck), trimmed of fat and sinews removed (your butcher can do this for you) | 2 garlic cloves | 1 piece of fresh ginger | 200ml/7fl oz light soy sauce | 4 teaspoons sesame oil | 3 large shallots | 4 heads of pak choy | 125g/4oz shiitake (or oyster) mushrooms | 6 teaspoons sesame seeds | 1 bunch of mint, freshly picked (if possible)

pan-fried duck breast with
crispy cabbage & sesame
soy dressing

(recipe on following page)

(recipe picture on previous pages)

pan-fried duck breast with crispy cabbage & sesame soy dressing

1   To make the dressing, deseed and finely chop the chile. Chop the ginger as finely as possible.

2   Top and tail, then shred the spring onions as finely as possible.

3   Combine all the dressing ingredients together in a small bowl and leave, covered, in the refrigerator. Allow at least 6 hours to infuse.

4   Preheat oven to 180°C (350°F) Gas Mark 4. Meanwhile, season the duck breasts. Heat a large heavy-based frying pan and when hot, add some oil. Seal the underside of the breasts, about 2 minutes.

5   When the duck is nicely colored, turn it skinside over and place the pan in the oven for about 10 minutes. At this stage the duck breasts should be crispy on the outside and pink in the middle. Allow to rest for 5 minutes before slicing.

6   To serve, arrange the shredded iceberg leaves in a neat pile on each plate with the crispy greens on top. Arrange the duck breast on top and serve the sauce in dipping bowls.

 Stir-Fried Ginger Noodles (see page 83) make a great side dish with this recipe.

ingredients 4 x 180g/6¼oz duck breasts, trimmed of sinew (your butcher can do this for you) ▌ a little sunflower oil for frying ▌ salt and freshly ground black pepper ▌ FOR THE DRESSING 1 dried red chile ▌ 1 piece of fresh ginger (about 20g/¾oz), peeled ▌ 2 spring onions ▌ 6 tablespoons light soy sauce ▌ 8 tablespoons rice vinegar ▌ 1 tablespoon superfine sugar ▌ 2 tablespoons pure sesame oil ▌ FOR THE GARNISH 6 large iceberg lettuce leaves, finely shredded ▌ 2 heads of young cabbage, finely shredded, deep-fried, and drained on paper towels

sauté of beef with limes, salt, and pepper

1 Peel and cut the onions into strips. Heat some oil
   in a large heavy-based frying pan and fry the onions
   (do not allow them to color), about 2 minutes. Set
   aside.

2 Heat some more oil in the saucepan and, when
   hot, fry the steak strips quickly until almost sealed,
   about 2 minutes. Mix in the onion strips. Add
   the soy sauce and mix together quickly, allowing the
   sauce to coat the meat and onions and thicken.

3 To serve, cut the limes in half and arrange on plates
   with the steak mixture. Put some salt and pepper
   together at the top of each plate. To really enjoy
   this dish, each person should squeeze their lime half
   onto the salt and pepper and mix it into a paste.
   The beef-onion mixture is dipped into the paste.

 Sticky Rice (see page 60) makes the perfect accompaniment to this dish.

ingredients 2 large onions ▎ a little sunflower oil for frying ▎ 700g/1lb 6oz sirloin steak, fat-free and cut into strips ▎
90ml/6 tablespoons sweet soy sauce ▎ 2 limes ▎ 4 tablespoons each: salt and freshly ground black pepper

barbecued pork ribs with hoisin sauce

1   To make the marinade, first peel the shallots. Slice the shallots and then the lemongrass into thin rings. Mix all the ingredients for the marinade together in a large bowl.

2   Add the ribs, coat thoroughly in the mixture, and leave to marinate for at least 6 hours in a warm place before cooking.

3   Preheat oven to 150°C (300°F) Gas Mark 2. Place the ribs in a roasting pan and bake for about 2 hours, depending on size, until cooked. Check the oven regularly and turn the ribs occasionally as they cook.

4   While the ribs are roasting, prepare the garnish. Deseed and cut the peppers into strips and peel and slice the onions. Cut the spring onions in half, then in half again lengthwise.

5   Heat a wok and, when hot, add the sunflower oil. Stir fry the vegetables in the wok until cooked, about 2 minutes. Add the ribs and stir in the soy sauce. Cook quickly to allow the sauce to thicken slightly, about 1 minute; thoroughly coat the ribs.

6   To serve, stack the ribs high on each plate. Serve with Sticky Rice and finger bowls.

ingredients   1.5kg/3lb baby back spare ribs, cut into sticks (your butcher can do this for you) ❙ Sticky Rice (see page 60), to serve ❙ FOR THE MARINADE 2 shallots ❙ 2 sticks of lemongrass ❙ 3 tablespoons rice vinegar ❙ 6 tablespoons hoisin sauce ❙ 4 tablespoons water ❙ 1 tablespoon light soy sauce ❙ salt and freshly ground black pepper to taste ❙ FOR THE GARNISH 2 red peppers ❙ 3 green peppers ❙ 2 onions ❙ 2 bunches spring onions ❙ 2 x 50g/2oz packets of baby corn ❙ a little sunflower oil for frying ❙ 8 tablespoons sweet soy sauce

crispy quail with watercress

1. To make the marinade, peel and finely slice the ginger, garlic, and shallot.

2. Combine all the marinade ingredients in a large bowl and pass the quail through, one at a time, to coat thoroughly. Place the quail on baking sheets.

3. Leave the quail to marinate in the refrigerator, covered, for at least 8 hours.

4. To cook the quail, place them in a steamer or on a cooling rack over a roasting tray filled with enough water to cover the base. Cover with foil and steam for 5 minutes.

5. Allow the quail to cool on the steamer tray or cooling rack, then refrigerate, covered, until needed.

6. To make the spiced flour, grind the coriander and cumin seeds together. Combine all the ingredients in a large shallow bowl.

7. Pass the quail through the spiced flour, then deep fry in a deep-fat fryer until crispy, about 2 minutes. Drain on kitchen paper.

8. While the quail are cooking, wash and divide the watercress into sprigs.

9. To serve, place two quail on each plate and garnish with a clump of watercress.

 Tamarind Sauce (see page 65) is an ideal accompaniment, while Stir-Fried Ginger Noodles (see page 83) complement this dish well.

ingredients 8 quail ▌ a little vegetable oil for deep frying ▌ FOR THE MARINADE 1 medium piece of fresh ginger ▌ 1 garlic clove ▌ 1 large shallot ▌ 5 tablespoons five spice powder ▌ 3 tablespoons sweet soy sauce ▌ 2 tablespoons demerara sugar ▌ 4 tablespoons Nuoc Cham (see page 57) ▌ 2 tablespoons rice vinegar ▌ 3 tablespoons caramel (see Sesame Banana Fritters, page 162) ▌ FOR THE SPICED FLOUR 1 tablespoon each: coriander and cumin seeds ▌ 4 tablespoons flour ▌ 1 tablespoon paprika ▌ 2 tablespoons potato flour ▌ 5 teaspoons chile powder ▌ 2 teaspoons ground black pepper ▌ 1 teaspoon salt ▌ FOR THE GARNISH 1 bunch watercress

teriyaki pork stew

1 In a shallow dish. mix together the teriyaki marinade, light soy, and oyster sauces. Add the dried chile and marinate the pork strips, covered, for 3 hours in the refrigerator.

2 Peel and finely chop the garlic, peel and finely slice the shallot, and peel and finely chop the ginger.

3 Cut the peppers in half, deseed, and finely slice them.

4 Wipe the mushrooms, remove the stalks, and finely slice.

5 Shred the spring onions and finely chop the cilantro.

6 In a large bowl, combine all the vegetables.

7 Preheat oven to 180–190°C (350–375°F) Gas Mark 4–5. Place the pork strips in a slightly oiled roasting pan and roast for about 10 minutes until golden. Allow to cool slightly, then slice into small strips.

8 Add some oil to a hot wok and fry the vegetables until just crispy, about 3 minutes. Add the pork, stir in the sweet soy sauce, and fry until the meat is cooked, about 5 minutes.

Serve this dish with Sticky Rice, Wok-seared Green, or Spicy Herbed Leaf Salad (see pages 60, 86, and 93). Buy rindless and boneless pork as this will marinate more easily. It will also be easier to slice after cooking.

ingredients 4 x 200g/7oz pork strips, boneless and rindless (your butcher can do this for you) | 1 garlic clove | 1 large shallot | 1 medium piece of fresh ginger | 2 red peppers and 1 green pepper | 130g/4½oz shiitake mushrooms | 1 bunch of spring onions | 1 bunch of cilantro, freshly picked (if possible) | a little sunflower oil for roasting and frying | 120ml/4floz sweet soy sauce | FOR THE MARINADE 4 tablespoons teriyaki marinade | 1 tablespoon each: light soy and oyster sauces | 1 dried chile

desserts & drinks

"In the evening, one sits on the terraces

of recently constructed cafés, luxurious

and comfortable, where one takes a slow

aperitif, while watching the bustling

crowds."

[On Saigon]
Au Tonkin: Journal d'un sous-officier d'infantrie de Marien,
A. Bodier & H. Bodier, 1890

passion fruit & pomegranate tart

1   To make the tart crust, in a large bowl, soften the butter. In a separate bowl, sift together the flour and sugar. Beat an egg into the flour–sugar mixture, add the butter, and beat together again to form the dough. Cover in plastic wrap and refrigerate for 1 hour.

2   Preheat oven to 190°C (375°F) Gas Mark 5. On a floured surface, roll out the dough to just larger than a 9-inch tart dish. Leave to rest, uncovered, for a further 30 minutes. Use the dough to line the dish.

3   Bake the crust in the center of the oven for about 30 minutes. When cool, separate the remaining egg and brush the crust with egg yolk. Bake again for 5–10 minutes until a crust has formed.

4   Reduce oven heat to 150°C (300°F) Gas Mark 2. Meanwhile, to make the filling, cut the pomegranate in half and scrape the seeds out into a large bowl. Split the seeds into pieces.

5   Add the remaining ingredients except for 2 tablespoons of passion fruit purée. Stir the filling to disperse the pomegranate seeds as widely as possible and pour into the cooled tart crust.

6   Bake the tart in the oven for about 1 hour or until it has set.

7   To serve, scrape the seeds from the 2 passion fruits into a large bowl. Split the seeds with a knife and combine with the remaining passion fruit purée to form a sauce. Cut the tart into wedges and garnish with sauce.

Fresh Vanilla Bean Ice Cream (see page 163) is a perfect accompaniment to this dessert. Passion fruit purée can usually be found frozen in most supermarkets. Alternatively, buy passion fruit juice and reduce by half over a low heat.

ingredients 1 pomegranate | 1½ cups heavy cream | 4 eggs | ¾ cup superfine sugar | 1⅓ cups passion fruit purée | FOR THE TART CRUST ½ pound (2 sticks) unsalted butter | 2½ cups flour, plus 6 tablespoons for rolling out | ¾ cup superfine sugar | 2 eggs | FOR THE GARNISH 2 passion fruits

spiced fruit salad

1   To make the syrup, place all the ingredients together
   in a large heavy-based saucepan. Gently simmer for
   about 15 minutes, stirring occasionally.

2   Allow the syrup to cool, then pass through a fine
   sieve into a bowl. Set aside.

3   Prepare the fruit as desired.

4   To serve, arrange the fruit around a serving platter
   or on individual plates. Try to mix the flavors and
   then drizzle syrup over the top.

 *In this recipe, the fruit can vary according
to seasonal and market availability. Be
prepared to change fruit combinations from time to
time. Serve with ice cream in the summer.*

ingredients   selection of enough fresh fruit for 4 people, such as pineapples, papayas, star fruits, melons, pink
grapefruits, lychees, oranges (blood oranges if in season), mangoes, plums, pears, or pomegranates | FOR THE SPICED SYRUP
3¹/₃ cups water | 6 whole dried star anise | 4 vanilla beans | rinds of 1 lemon and 1 lime | 2 cinnamon sticks | 8 cloves
| 2¹/₃ cups superfine sugar

sweet coconut rice with
stewed mango, mandarin, & ginger

1   To make the coconut rice, preheat oven to 160°C
    (325°F) Gas Mark 3. Split the vanilla bean in half
    lengthwise. Place in a large heavy-based casserole.
    Scrape out the seeds and then add to the casserole
    with the beans. Add the coconut and semi-skimmed
    milk, heavy cream, sugar, star anise, and coconut.
    Bring to a boil. Leave to simmer for 10 minutes,
    stirring occasionally.

2   Use a slotted spoon to remove the vanilla pod and
    star anise.

3   Quickly wash the rice (do not soak) and add to the
    simmering milk. Leave to simmer for another 5
    minutes. Cover the casserole with foil (this prevents
    a skin from forming) and bake the rice in the oven
    for about 20 minutes until set. Leave to cool until
    the rice is warm, not hot.

4   Meanwhile, to make the garnish, peel and dice the
    mango. Peel, segment, and remove all pith from the
    mandarins. Peel and finely dice the ginger. Combine
    all three in a large bowl.

5   In a large heavy-based saucepan, warm the syrup.
    Add the fruit and ginger, then remove from the heat
    and leave to marinate for about 1 hour, covered in
    the refrigerator.

6   To serve, line 4 small ring molds (about 5cm/2in
    diameter) with melted butter and toasted dried
    coconut. Fill the rings with the warm rice and turn
    out onto a serving dish. Place marinated fruit
    around the dish and drizzle lightly with syrup.
    Garnish with small sprigs of mint.

 *Pickled red ginger is available at Asian
grocery stores and some supermarkets.*

ingredients 1 vanilla bean | 1 cup coconut milk | 2 cups each: lowfat milk and heavy cream | ⅓ cup superfine sugar
| 2 whole dried star anise | 4 tablespoons toasted dried coconut (toast on a baking sheet under a broiler) | 2 cups (uncooked)
short grain rice | a little melted butter | FOR THE GARNISH 1 ripe mango | 2 mandarins (or small oranges) | 1 stem pickled
red ginger | 1 quantity of spiced syrup (see Spiced Fruit Salad, page 154) | 4 small sprigs of mint, freshly picked (if possible)

caramelized banana & coconut puddings

1 Preheat oven to 140°C (275°F) Gas Mark 1. Meanwhile, split the vanilla beans in half lengthwise and use a sharp knife to scrape the seeds into a small heavy-based saucepan. Add the pods and the coconut milk and bring to a boil, stirring occasionally.

2 Pour the mixture into a large heatproof bowl. Whisk in the egg yolks, stir in the dried coconut, and leave to cool, about 30 minutes.

3 Peel and thinly slice the bananas. Arrange about 5 thin slices in the base of individual molds. Top each mold with a tablespoon of caramel.

4 Use another mold to trim the bread into rounds. Dip 4 rounds into the coconut milk mixture and layer on top of the banana in each mold.

5 Add another layer of banana and top with a tablespoon of the coconut milk mixture.

6 Dip 4 more rounds of bread into the coconut milk mixture. Place these on top of the sliced bananas. Top with more sliced banana and the coconut mixture as before. Repeat until all the banana slices and bread rounds have been used up, spooning some of the coconut milk on top as the layers build up and finishing with a layer of dipped bread.

7 Spoon the remaining coconut milk over each mold, and cover with discs of parchment paper and then foil. Bake in the center of the oven for about 20 minutes until golden and set.

8 In a small heavy-based saucepan, mix the remaining caramel with the heavy cream. Warm through, stirring continuously.

9 To serve, turn the puddings out onto serving dishes and top with the caramel sauce. Serve with Coconut Sorbet.

ingredients   2 vanilla beans ▌ 3$\frac{1}{2}$ cups coconut milk ▌ 3 egg yolks ▌ 1 cup dried coconut, toasted ▌ 4 bananas ▌ 4 tablespoons caramel (see Sesame Banana Fritters, page 162) ▌ 12 slices of thin white bread (or 6 slices thick bread), sliced through the middle ▌ 2$\frac{1}{2}$ tablespoons heavy cream ▌ Coconut Sorbet (see page 166), to serve

chocolate & cashew nut brownies

1 Preheat oven to 180°C (350°F) Gas Mark 4. Meanwhile, over a bain-marie (a bowl over a saucepan of hot water), melt the cocoa powder, 90g/3oz chocolate and butter together.

2 In a separate bowl, whisk the egg and superfine sugar until soft peaks form, about 2 minutes, using a handheld mixer. Fold into the mixture.

3 Roast the cashew nuts on a baking sheet for 5–10 minutes. Chop into small pieces and add to the chocolate mixture with the flour; fold in until the mixture is combined.

4 Transfer the mixture to 4 small greased ring molds (about 5cm/2in diameter). Bake for 15–20 minutes or until just done (slightly sticky in the middle). To check this, place a knife through the middle of the brownie and if a little of the mixture sticks to the knife, it is ready.

5 To serve, make up a quantity of caramel and fold in the remaining milk chocolate to darken and sweeten the caramel. Serve the brownies with chocolate ice cream.

The brownies can be made in advance. While still warm (not hot), cover with plastic wrap. When required, remove the plastic wrap and microwave for 20–30 seconds.

ingredients 1 tablespoon cocoa powder ❙ 120g/4oz milk chocolate ❙ ¼ cup unsalted butter, plus extra for greasing ❙ 1 egg ❙ ½ cup superfine sugar ❙ ⅓ cup cashew nuts ❙ ½ cup flour ❙ caramel (see Sesame Banana Fritters, page 162) ❙ chocolate ice cream, to serve

sesame banana fritters

1 In a large heavy-based frying pan, dry roast the sesame seeds until brown, about 4 minutes. Leave to cool, then grind.

2 Cover a stainless steel baking sheet with silicone paper.

3 To make the caramel, place the sugar in a large heavy-based saucepan, add the water and bring to a boil over medium heat. Leave to caramelize, about 10–15 minutes. The caramel will reach a temperature of almost 180°C/350°F, so care and attention are required at this stage.

4 When the caramel is ready, pour it onto the baking sheet. Sprinkle with about 2 tablespoons of the ground sesame seeds (enough to coat the fritters) and allow to cool.

5 When the caramel is cold, break it into small pieces and grind to the consistency of sugar. Place in an airtight plastic container and refrigerate.

6 Place tempura batter flour into a large bowl and whisk in 12 tablespoons cold water .

7 Cut each banana into three equal pieces. Roll each one through the remaining flour, then through the batter. Deep fry until cooked and crispy, about 4 minutes.

8 Place the caramelized sesame crystals and the honey in a stainless steel bowl and stir together. Add the fritters and roll them around in the bowl until they are completely coated in the mixture.

9 Serve several banana segments with a scoop of vanilla ice cream. Sprinkle with the remaining sesame powder and serve immediately.

To caramelize sugar correctly, invest in a proper sugar thermometer. Do not leave the pan unattended when the sugar is caramelizing. Tempura flour lends a different texture to this recipe and is well worth finding.

ingredients 3 tablespoons sesame seeds | 12 tablespoons cold water | 1⅓ cups tempura batter flour, available from Asian stores | 4 bananas | oil for frying | 8 tablespoons honey | 4 scoops Fresh Vanilla Bean Ice Cream (see page 163) | FOR THE CARAMEL ⅔ cup superfine sugar | 4 tablespoons water

fresh vanilla bean ice cream

1   Pour the milk and cream into a large heavy-based saucepan and heat through.

2   Split the vanilla beans in half lengthways and scrape the seeds out into the milk. Add the beans and stir to combine. Bring the mixture to a boil.

3   Meanwhile, in a large heatproof bowl, whisk together the egg yolks and superfine sugar until soft peaks form, about 2 minutes, with a handheld mixer.

4   Pour the milk mixture onto the egg and sugar mixture, stirring continuously, then return the mixture to the saucepan.

5   Slowly cook the mixture over low heat, stirring, about 2 minutes. Do not allow to boil. Pass the mixture through a large sieve into a bowl.

6   Leave the mixture to cool completely before churning to make ice cream (see note).

If an ice cream machine is not available, place the cold mixture in a stainless steel bowl in the freezer, uncovered, and stir every 10 minutes with a stainless steel spoon. Although this method will not give you the same taste as homemade ice cream made in a machine, it is the next best thing.

ingredients   2 cups milk ▎ 1 cup heavy cream ▎ 2 vanilla beans ▎ 10 egg yolks ▎ 1 cup superfine sugar

sesame banana fritters

(recipe on page 162)

honey & ginger ice cream

1 Pour the milk and cream into a large heavy-based saucepan and heat through. Stir in the ginger and bring the mixture to a boil.

2 In a large heatproof bowl, whisk together the sugar and egg yolks until soft peaks form, about 2 minutes, with a handheld mixer.

3 Pour the milk mixture onto the egg and sugar mixture, stirring continuously, then return the mixture to the saucepan.

4 Slowly cook the mixture over low heat, stirring, about 2 minutes. Do not allow to boil. Pass the mixture through a large sieve into a bowl.

5 Leave the mixture to cool completely, then stir in the honey and combine.

6 Churn in the same way as for Fresh Vanilla Bean Ice Cream (see page 163).

ingredients 2 cups milk ❘ 1 cup heavy cream ❘ 3 tablespoons peeled and finely grated fresh ginger ❘ ¼ cup superfine sugar ❘ 10 egg yolks ❘ 3 tablespoons honey

coconut sorbet

1 Place the sugar and water in a large heavy-based saucepan. Bring to a boil and simmer for 5 minutes, stirring occasionally. If you wish to spice the mixture up, you can add a cinnamon stick, cloves, star anise, or even a little fruit peel, but be careful not to add too much as coconut should be the dominant flavor in this recipe.

2 While the mixture is still warm, stir in the coconut milk and leave to cool.

3 Churn, following the same method as for Fresh Vanilla Bean Ice Cream (see page 163).

 Coconut milk is readily available at most supermarkets.

ingredients 2 cups superfine sugar ❘ 2 cups water ❘ ½ cinnamon stick (optional) ❘ 1 clove (optional) ❘ 1 dried star anise or the peel from 1 orange (optional) ❘ 2 cups coconut milk

lemon & lime meringue

1 In a large heavy-based saucepan, place ½ cup sugar, the rind and juice of 2 limes, and the lemongrass. Pour in the water and bring the mixture to a boil, stirring occasionally. Remove from the heat and stir in the cornstarch before the mixture cools so that it dissolves. Leave to infuse for 1 hour in a warm place.

2 In a large bowl, soften the butter and fold in the egg yolks. Combine with the infusion.

3 Pour the mixture into 4 molds (see note), leaving space at the top of each for the meringue.

4 In a large bowl, whisk the egg whites with the remaining sugar until stiff peaks form. Grate the rind from the remaining lime and fold this into the meringue. Refrigerate until set, about 2 hours.

5 Place the individual molds inside a serving dish. Top with meringue and smooth the surface of each one with a palette knife. Place under a broiler to brown the tops quickly or use a blow torch. (Do not allow the mousse to become runny.)

6 Garnish with crystallized lemon or lime rind.

 Use the same molds as for Chocolate & Lemongrass Mousse (see page 170). A little lemon sorbet served on the side adds a pleasant sharpness to this dessert.

ingredients ⅔ cup superfine sugar ▮ 3 limes ▮ 2 sticks of lemongrass, finely chopped ▮ ⅓ cup water ▮ 2 tablespoons cornstarch ▮ 2 tablespoons unsalted butter ▮ 2 eggs, separated ▮ FOR THE GARNISH handful crystallized lemon or lime rind

chocolate & lemongrass mousse

1   Finely chop the lemongrass into small pieces or finely grind in a food processor or mortar and pestle.

2   Pour the milk into a large heavy-based saucepan, add the lemongrass, and bring to a boil. Remove from the heat and leave to infuse for 1 hour.

3   Break the chocolate into cubes and melt in a bain-marie or a microwave. Soften the gelatin in a small bowl filled with cold water and stir it into the chocolate until dissolved.

4   In a medium bowl, whisk the egg yolks and sugar. Semiwhip the heavy cream in a separate bowl.

5   Whisk the egg-sugar mixture into the milk. Return to low heat, stirring continuously to slowly cook the egg until the mixture has slightly thickened. Remove from the heat and stir in the melted chocolate. Leave to cool slightly.

6   Pass the mixture through a sieve to remove the lemongrass. Allow to cool completely.

7   Slowly fold in the heavy cream (do not overwhip the cream or it will separate). Pour the mousse into molds (see note) and leave to set in the refrigerator, about 2 hours.

8   Just prior to serving, make the sauce, juicing the lemons into a small heavy-based saucepan. Reduce by two-thirds over a low heat. Add a little sugar to taste. Thicken with cornstarch as desired.

9   To serve, turn each mousse out onto a plate. Garnish with caramelized lemon rind and drizzle with sauce.

 The molds used in this recipe are 7cm/3in in diameter and 3cm/1½ in high. They can be either stainless steel, ceramic, or plastic, but not aluminum. Remember that the finer you chop the lemongrass, the more flavor the mousse will have.

ingredients 3 sticks of lemongrass **|** 1 cup milk **|** 140g/4½oz milk chocolate **|** 1 packet gelatin **|** 2 egg yolks **|** ¼ cup superfine sugar **|** ⅔ cup heavy cream **|** FOR THE GARNISH 2 lemons **|** superfine sugar and cornstarch, to taste **|** handful crystallized lemond rinds

kaffir lime brûlée

1 Using the fine side of the grater, remove the rind from the limes. Juice the limes.

2 In a coffee grinder, food processor, or mortar and pestle, grind the lime leaves to a fine powder.

3 In a bowl, combine the lime juice and rind and the powdered lime leaves with the remaining ingredients. Leave, covered, to infuse for about 6 hours in the refrigerator.

4 Preheat oven to 120°C (250°F) Gas Mark ½. Meanwhile, transfer the brûlée mixture to small shallow molds. Line a roasting pan with newspaper, add the molds, and fill the pan with water to a height of about one inch. Bake for about 1 hour until set. Leave to cool and set in the refrigerator, about 2 hours.

5 To serve, sprinkle with demerara sugar and caramelize with either a blow torch or under a broiler for a few minutes. Leave to cool slightly before serving to allow the glaze to harden.

 The brûlée mixture can be made up a day in advance and left, covered, in the refrigerator to infuse.

ingredients 2 kaffir limes or 3 ordinary limes ❚ 3 lime leaves or the zest of 1 lime, if leaves unavailable (do not add lime juice) ❚ 1 cup heavy cream ❚ ¼ cup superfine sugar ❚ 5 egg yolks ❚ FOR THE GLAZE demerara sugar

opposite: *assorted cocktails*

bam-bou kiwi fruit

1 Use a sharp knife to peel the kiwi fruit and cut them into small pieces. Place in the blender and purée, about 1 minute.

2 Pour the purée into the glass of a cocktail shaker, then fill it with ice. Add the gin, Krupnik, and Midori, place the lid on top and shake, about 30 seconds.

3 Fill a tumbler with ice and strain the cocktail contents onto the ice.

4 Garnish with a slice of star fruit and two cocktail straws, then serve immediately.

ingredients 2 kiwi fruit **|** crushed ice (enough to fill a 600ml/1 pint cocktail shaker) **|** 15ml/½fl oz Bombay Sapphire gin **|** 4 teaspoons Krupnik (honey-flavored vodka) **|** 4 teaspoons Midori **|** TO GARNISH slice of star fruit **|** EQUIPMENT blender **|** coktail shaker **|** cocktail strainer

saigon cooler

1 In the mortar and pestle, mash the raspberries into a smooth purée.

2 Fill the shaker with ice and add all the ingredients except for the soda water and garnish. Place the lid on top and shake vigorously, about 30 seconds.

3 Fill a highball glass with fresh ice and strain the cocktail in slowly. Fill to the top with soda water.

4 Garnish with either a lime wedge or slice of star fruit and serve immediately.

ingredients 20–30 fresh raspberries **|** crushed ice (enough to fill a 600ml/1 pint cocktail shaker) **|** 25ml/1fl oz gin **|** 15ml/½fl oz Chambord (wild raspberry liqueur) **|** 4 teaspoons cranberry juice **|** 2 teaspoons simple syrup **|** soda water **|** TO GARNISH lime wedge or slice of star fruit **|** EQUIPMENT mortar and pestle **|** cocktail shaker **|** cocktail strainer

Asian passion

1   Before you begin to make this cocktail, place a
    martini glass in the freezer until it is nicely chilled,
    about 10 minutes.

2   Fill the glass of the cocktail shaker with ice, add the
    remaining ingredients apart from the lemon, and
    put the lid on. Shake vigorously, about 1 minute.

3   Strain the cocktail into the chilled glass and garnish
    with a lemon twist.

ingredients crushed ice (enough to fill a 600ml/1 pint cocktail shaker) | 2 teaspoons passion fruit purée (see note,
page 153) | 25ml/1fl oz gin | 15ml/1/2fl oz Limoncello (or the juice from 1 lemon) | 2 teaspoons passion fruit or simple
syrup | TO GARNISH lemon twist | EQUIPMENT cocktail shaker | cocktail strainer

citron caipiroska

1   Place the sugar in a tumbler. Cut the lime into small
    wedges and add to the glass.

2   Mash the lime and sugar together with the pestle
    until the sugar has completely dissolved.

3   Add the vodka and stir until all the ingredients have
    blended together.

4   Top the glass with crushed ice until overflowing;
    gently stir.

5   This cocktail requires no garnish. Just add two short
    cocktail straws and serve immediately.

ingredients 3–4 brown sugar cubes (3–4 teaspoons demerara sugar) | 1 lime | 50ml/2fl oz Absolut Citron | 300ml/1/2
pint crushed ice | EQUIPMENT mortar and pestle | bar spoon

bam-bou bellini

1   First peel (if necessary), then purée your chosen
    fruit. If the fruit isn't quite ripe, try adding half a
    teaspoon sugar.

2   Fill half of the cocktail shaker with crushed ice. Add
    roughly 50ml/2fl oz of fruit purée. Slowly pour in
    the champagne and gently stir for about 10
    seconds.

3   Strain the cocktail into a champagne flute and serve
    immediately.

ingredients fresh fruit, such as raspberries, strawberries, or kiwi fruit | ½ teaspoon sugar (optional) | crushed ice (enough
to fill a 600ml/1 pint cocktail shaker) | 125ml/4fl oz champagne | EQUIPMENT food processor or blender | cocktail shaker | bar
spoon | cocktail strainer

Hanoi fizz

1   Fill a champagne flute halfway with champagne,
    then slowly spoon in the passion fruit purée.

2   Hold the champagne flute at a 45-degree angle and
    slowly pour in the Chambord.

3   If necessary, top up with more champagne and serve
    immediately.

ingredients about 125ml/4fl oz champagne | 25ml/1fl oz passion fruit purée (see note, page 153) | ½ teaspoon sugar
(optional) | 25ml/1fl oz Chambord (wild raspberry liqueur) EQUIPMENT food processor or blender | bar spoon

lychee cooler

1 Squeeze the juice from half of the lime, then fill a highball glass with crushed ice. Add the vodka and lime juice.

2 Fill the glass about three-quarters full with lychee juice, then fill to the top with soda water.

3 Garnish with a slice of star fruit to give the cocktail an exotic look and serve immediately.

ingredients 1 lime | crushed ice (enough to fill a highball glass) | 50ml/2fl oz Absolut vodka | 100ml/4fl oz lychee | soda water | TO GARNISH slice of star fruit | EQUIPMENT juicer

exotic fruit punch (non-alcoholic)

1 Fill the glass half of the shaker with ice and pour in the fruit juices.

2 Rinse and hull the strawberries; purée in either a blender or pestle and mortar. Add the strawberries to the juices.

3 Shake the cocktail vigorously and strain into a tall glass filled with ice.

4 Cut the lime into quarters, squeeze one quarter into the cocktail, and use the other as a garnish. Serve immediately with long straws.

ingredients crushed ice (enough to fill a 600ml/1 pint cocktail shaker) | 50ml/2fl oz guava juice | 50ml/2fl oz lychee juice | 50ml/2fl oz cranberry juice | 10 strawberries | ½ fresh lime | EQUIPMENT cocktail shaker | blender | mortar and pestle | cocktail strainer

red room sling

1 Fill the cocktail shaker with ice and add all the
   ingredients except for the orange juice and garnish.
   Place the lid on top and shake vigorously, about
   30 seconds.

2 Fill a highball glass with fresh ice, strain the cocktail
   onto the ice, and top with orange juice.

3 To garnish, take a slice of orange, skewer it onto a
   cocktail stick with a cherry, and place over the rim
   of the glass. Serve immediately with a long straw.

ingredients crushed ice (enough to fill a 600ml/1 pint cocktail shaker) | 25ml/1fl oz gin | 2 teaspoons DOM Benedictine
| 2 teaspoons Cointreau | 15ml/½fl oz Cherry Brandy | 15ml/½fl oz passion fruit purée (see note, page 153) | 2 teaspoons
Grenadine | fresh orange juice, to top | TO GARNISH orange slice and cocktail cherry | EQUIPMENT cocktail shaker | cocktail strainer

the lotus runner

1 Fill the cocktail shaker with ice. Add all the
   ingredients apart from the garnish. Place the lid on
   top and shake vigorously, about 30 seconds.

2 Strain the contents of the shaker into a martini
   glass, garnish with an orange twist, and serve
   immediately.

ingredients crushed ice (enough to fill a 600ml/1 pint cocktail shaker) | 25ml/1fl oz vodka | 15ml/½fl oz Grand Marnier
| 2 teaspoons Orgeat Almond syrup (or substitute Amaretto and reduce the amount to 1 teaspoon) | 4 teaspoons unsweetened
coconut purée | TO GARNISH 1 orange twist | EQUIPMENT cocktail shaker | cocktail strainer

menu suggestions

"Each guest, armed with a pair of ivory

chopsticks and a porcelain spoon, had before

him a small plate, a bowl full of rice and a

tiny cup for receiving rice wine."

Notes sur la Vie Francaise en Cochinchine, Pierre Nicolas, 1778

MENU 1 ⟨⟩ the summer buffet

This buffet is designed to satisfy 10 to 12 people, and would be ideal as a summer lunch as the dishes are all quite light. Most of the recipes can be prepared in advance, with just a short time required for last-minute reheating or quick frying. If you are expecting vegetarian guests you could replace the chicken or lamb dish with Mushroom and Rice-Stuffed Cabbage. Serve with non-alcoholic Exotic Fruit Punch and dry white wines.

- Crispy Spring Roll with Prawns, Pork, and Mushrooms
- Cha-Ca Monkfish with Turmeric, Dill, and Onion
- Sesame Lamb and Shiitake Sauté with Mint and Shallots
- Caramelized Ginger Chicken
- Wok-Seared Greens
- Spicy Noodle Salad
- Sticky Rice (optional)

- Sesame Banana Fritters
- Spiced Fruit Salad

MENU 2 ✺ the banquet

The heavier dishes on this menu make it well suited for an evening buffet that would serve about 20 people. If you have fewer, or more, people to feed, add or subtract dishes to your tastes. Start with finger food like the Fresh Soft Spring Roll with Chicken, Rice Noodles, Mint & Coriander, Shrimp on Sugar Cane, and Muc-Nhoi Stuffed Squid. Next, bring out the Vietnamese Hot Pot and Coconut Curried Vegetables, which will make a nice change of pace and help to clear the palate before serving the more substantial main dishes. Sticky Rice can be brought out with the hot pot and curried vegetables. The desserts can all be prepared in advance. Serve with a mix of dry white and full-bodied red wines. Be sure to put out several finger bowls of lemon water, and offer a choice of chopsticks and forks, along with spoons for the hot pot.

- Fresh Soft Spring Roll with Chicken, Rice Noodles, Mint and Cilantro
- Shrimp on Sugar Cane
- Muc-Nhoi Stuffed Squid

- Vietnamese Hot Pot with Beef, Prawns and Squid
- Coconut Curried Vegetables
- Sticky Rice

- Grilled Chicken Brochettes with Lemongrass Noodles
- Barbecued Pork Ribs with Hoisin Sauce
- Teriyaki Pork Stew
- Chicken and Cashew Stir-Fry
- Sauté of Beef with Limes, Salt, and Pepper
- Stir-Fried Ginger Noodles

- Lemon and Lime Meringue
- Passionfruit and Pomegranate Tart
- Chocolate and Cashew Nut Brownies

MENU 3 ✺ the simple dinner party

This three-course menu would serve 6 to 8 people and is a good one for trying out some of the easier recipes. The starters can be made in advance. The sauce for the Farchiew Pork Fillet can also be made earlier in the day to save time, and the Sesame Lamb can likewise be marinated beforehand. That leaves you free to focus on the Five-Spiced Cod. The desserts can also be largely prepared in advance, minimizing the time spent in the kitchen while your guests are at the table.

- Fresh Soft Spring Roll with Chicken, Rice Noodles, Mint, and Cilantro
- Peppered Tuna with Sour Tomato and Lemon

- Farchiew Pork Fillet
- Five-Spiced Cod with Tamarind and Herbs
- Sesame Lamb and Shiitake Sauté with Mint and Shallots
- Sticky Rice
- Wok-Seared Greens
- Fried Eggplant and Tomato Tofu (optional)

- Chocolate and Lemongrass Mousse
- Spiced Fruit Salad

MENU 4 ❂ the advanced four-course dinner party

Try out this menu once you've had time to become familiar with the recipes and are ready to make a truly impressive dinner. This one serves 12 people, but can be tailored to serve fewer guests by dropping whichever dishes you prefer. Remember that each of the recipes is designed to provide four portions, together with a rice or noodle and vegetable accompaniment so you can easily work out how many dishes you want. Sticky Rice is always popular and can be eaten with just about all the dishes, so it may be worthwhile making an extra serving. After dessert, serve jasmine or mint tea, or, for those with stronger constitutions, sake.

- Crispy Spring Roll with Prawns, Pork, and Mushrooms
- Sesame Prawns with Sour Green Mango Salad
- Crispy Smoked Chicken with Fragrant Greens

- Crab and Asparagus Soup
- Vietnamese Hot Pot with Beef, Prawns, and Squid

- Caramelized Ginger Chicken
- Grilled Fillet of Sole Wrapped in Banana Leaves
- Pan-Fried Duck Breast with Crispy Greens and Sesame Soy Dressing
- Curried Frogs' Legs
- Sticky Rice
- Stir-Fried Ginger Noodles
- Spicy Herbed Leaf Salad

- Passionfruit and Pomegranate Tart
- Chocolate and Cashew Nut Brownies
- Spiced Fruit Salad

INDEX

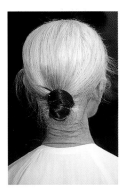

Acknowledgments

The publishers would like to thank Mark Read, Jan Dodd, Jane Donovan, Lovelock & Co, and Gwynn-fyl Lowe.

I would like to thank Chris Benians for his support and confidence in allowing me to write this book; Andy Magson for his kind and truthful words of wisdom over the past five years; all my kitchen team for their hard work and dedication in the setting up and vast improvement over the past 12 months, including Ben Martin, Juan Gonzalez, Roberto Campana, Oliver Vincent, Chris Beynnon, Mark Gilbert, Kien Pham, Ali Acka, Anthony Briggs, and Toni Reid; Jespal Soor, the head barman, for his cocktails; Katherine Ellis-Jones for all her running around after us; the Management team, Clive Gregory, Bruce Alexander, and Nikki Wilkerson, for allowing me to disrupt the restaurant during the photo shoots; Many thanks also to my main suppliers: George Allen (produce grocer), British Premium Meats, and Daily Fish Supplies. I would also like to thank Jean Cazals for teaching me life through a lens while sticking to a tight schedule during shooting, and everything David Mackintosh and Alex Black had to endure. As well as everybody else I've forgotten to mention. Thank you all so very much. *Mark Read*

For Marie-Ange and Clara . . . *Jean Cazals*

BAM-BOU is at 1 Percy Street, London W1P 0ET   Tel: 020 7323 9130